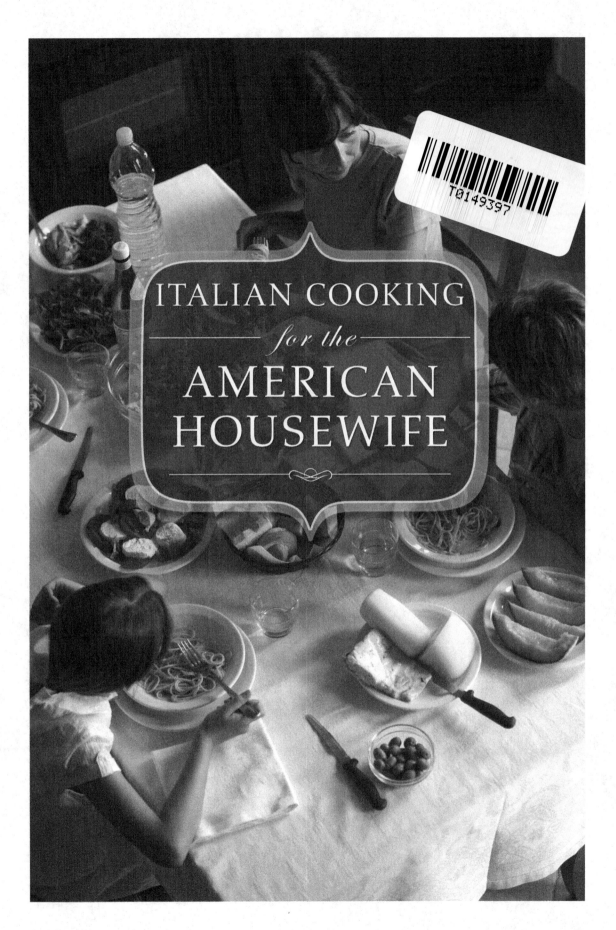

ITALIAN COOKING
for the
AMERICAN HOUSEWIFE

AuthorHouse™ LLC
1663 Liberty Drive
Bloomington, IN 47403
www.authorhouse.com
Phone: 1-800-839-8640

Published by AuthorHouse   09/11/2014

ISBN: 978-1-4969-3779-7 (sc)
ISBN: 978-1-4969-3778-0 (e)

ITALIAN COOKING FOR THE AMERICAN HOUSEWIFE

Italian Cooking 1: Mediterranean Cuisine

Paul Wichert

authorHOUSE®

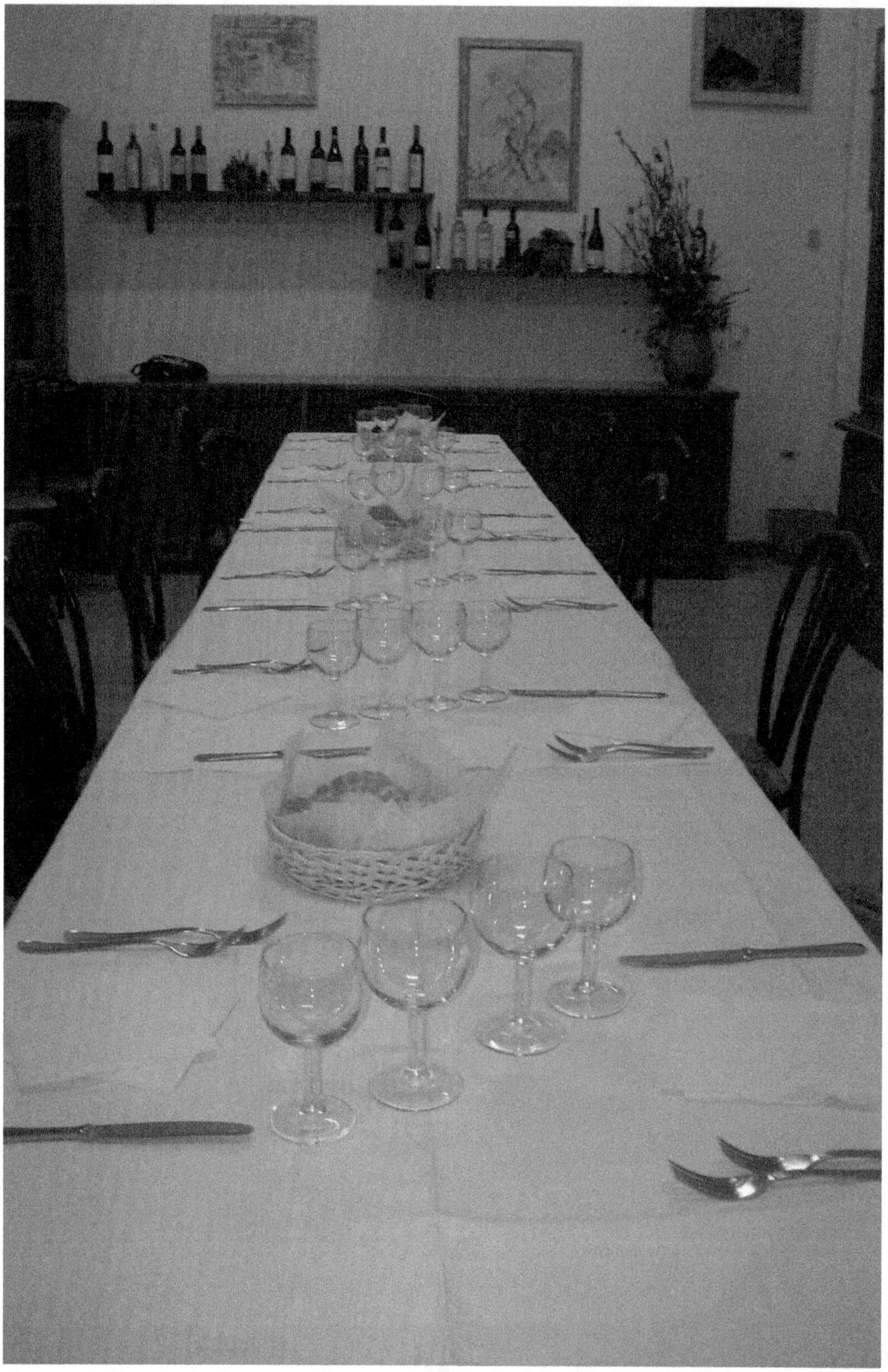

The long table is formally set for twelve people.

TABLE OF CONTENTS

1. Preface...viii
2. The principal's letter..1
3. Italian Cooking Vocabulary..18
4. The Recipes-Mediterranean cuisine..23
   - Antipasti...25
   - Primi...42
   - Seconde di pesce...74
   - Seconde di carne...83
   - Contourni...98
   - Dolce...107
5. Index of recipes..129
6. Appendix..131

PREFACE

The trip of a lifetime, going to Italy as eighth of nine culinary students, in a cultural exchange program to learn Italian cooking skills from Italian instructors in Italy, suddenly opened up to me while I was near graduation from the Great Lakes Culinary Institute in Traverse City, Michigan the culinary arts school affiliated with Northwestern Michigan College. A spokesman for the Italian Semester Abroad program was speaking to administrators at Great Lakes Culinary having traveled to many campuses promoting this cultural opportunity for college students across America. Originating in 2004, the Marco Polo organization first reigned in students from Monroe College in New York City, and soon thereafter from Paul Smith's College in New York on the 90-day Italian Culinary Tour of four regions.

Over a period of three months, from August 27th to November 27th, we lived in Italy and became immersed in their language and culture. The itinerary called for 4 weeks in southern Italy, 3 weeks in northern Italy on the eastern coast, followed by 3 weeks in the mountains, and finishing with 10 days in the city of Parma. The first region, Puglia in southern Italy, referred to as the heel of the boot was the host for our first months' stay as we learned the Italian language, attended professional cooking school, worked at restaurants in the city of Otranto, and took numerous fieldtrips along the Aegean Sea coast as far as the Ionian Sea.

This book, Italian Cooking for the American housewife, contains recipes from the Puglia region translated out of Italian into English. These are recipes we tried out at the cooking school, with the addition of selected dishes from restaurants in the local region. Menu plans from the school, from our resort and from the going away party have been included to provide the reader with a notion to pair certain courses together. At a going away party, the school gave us certificates for "A Course in Mediterranean Cuisine." For me, realizing how much I wanted to share this experience with others gave me strong feelings of motivation while making this translation. So each recipe may be simple enough to follow, while both the verbs and expressions are left with the sense of being straight out of the Italian. I wanted to bring Italy back with me, and try to bring a sense of familiarity to Mediterranean style Italian cooking.

Upon our arrival and at every turn, the Italian landscape marveled us, and the people enchanted us with their friendliness and willingness to reach common ground. Of course, we had to overcome our own cultural bias and accept events as they unfold while staying in the moment. In matters of the kitchen, our group had to agree with each other about dividing the labor, and reach a conclusion-to create a dish we wanted to set out on the table. To begin with an idea of what groceries have been placed on the counter, we use fresh chopped meats from the butcher which we might push into a meat grinder: veal, lamb, pork and beef were the most commonly used meats for this purpose. In this seaside hideaway, there are many different merchants selling fresh fish, octopus, squid, cuddlefish, black mussels, specialty clams called vognoles and other seafood catch. Farmers markets are open a few times a month where you can find whole cheeses, cured meats, eggs, fruit & nuts, vegetables, and fresh cut flowers. While the Italian city has a supermarket or two, the restaurant Smile at our resort has a pantry full of dry goods that are delivered by a commercial distributor at regular intervals. The wine is served chilled in glass pitchers; no need to open a new bottle, this wine is bought in bulk from a dealer who dispenses into your own jug.

Our host at the resort has a side operation, as owner of an olive oil production facility in a nearby location, the olive oil on our table is his own brand. As described in "the letter from the principal" the two main ingredients of the Mediterranean diet are olive oil and wine, grown and produced locally, used to supplement their daily pasta and bring together the various ingredients which make up these recipes.
On the table is olive oil with red hot chili pepper flakes warmed by the sun and slightly reddish in color.

A typical Mediterranean meal begins with fresh bread and olive oil for dipping, choice of pasta and meat or fish. Oftentimes the menu is set up for you to pick two dishes, one first course selection, and one second course selection. More elaborate meals include salad as antipasto and sometimes small plate portions as antipasto. Lunch and dinner beverages are bottled water, both natural and fizzy, and wine usually red wine; although Americans often ask for Coke and orange Fanta. Dessert course may be cake, custard filled pastry, panna cotta or seasonal fresh fruit. Meals are finished with expresso or cappuccino. For anyone who wants gelato that is a reason to stroll along the city lane to the gelato shoppe.

In the cooking school we had to make a few cultural adjustments to fully appreciate making fresh pasta daily as part of our routine, and to understand how the Italians make risotto and why they go to such great lengths to do so. Every day ingredients: the dairy, cheeses, and flour used in baking are all a little different from that in the United States. The milk is a little creamier; the cheeses are famous and made by artisans regionally; the flour comes in grades similar to cake flour, pastry flour and all purpose plus the yellow grain wheat flour known as semolina. There is also the appreciation of Italian culture, as we lounged for long hours taking in the family style meals, eating the six to seven course meals we prepared, one course at a time, sipping water and drinking the wine, talking and laughing as the hot days turned into warm cool evenings.

After school and a refreshing meal, we would walk down the city streets of Otranto exploring the shops and night life for an hour and a half before meeting at the taxi stand where our chauffeur would pick us up in the Mercedes. The driver returned us safely to our resort, a vast acreage with over 100 bungalows, family friendly, right next door to vacationers and their relatives, taking advantage of the resort's nightly entertainment, music and dancing which started after dark around 9:00 pm and went to 11:00 pm when the children got tired. The disc jockey and his partner moved the party to a small patio behind the snack bar and the party continued until 1:00 am.

School started at 8:30 am in a computer lab situated near the employee quarters. I would be up by 7:30 am in order to grab an expresso and croissant for breakfast in the snack bar. A college student from the nearby university did student teaching with our group as she is an education major specializing in multi-language learning. Somedays she took us on a field trip, such as farmers market, or historical tour through the city where she attends college. Generally, we had from 10:30 to noon to ourselves and then met up by the front office to get a lift to the local restaurants where we shadowed the cook during lunch shift. Smile is the name of the restaurant at our resort. It was the first restaurant that I had an opportunity to work during lunch shifts. The head cook became my friend right away after I learned how to ask his name. He always let me know what the specials were for today's meal, and let me do some preparations so he had it all together. There were three American culinary students to a group to help the cook and the girls who completed my group came from Monroe College in New York City. At the end of a week, the groups rotated to different restaurants and another group helped out at the Smile Ristorante. I worked for the cooks at Atlantis ristorante, La Fernanda ristorante, and the Da Ivo family ristorante during our time in Puglia. Often times, I take notes to remember what the cook is making, take snapshots, and try to get a feel for what the cook has to do every day. The chauffeur arrives at the end of the shift to return us to the Resort and we get a respite until class begins at the Professional Cooking School in the city starting by 3:00 pm. And so, another day unfolds to learn these cooking lessons and the recipes which are provided in this cookbook. Our chef has help from a translator who goes over each recipe before we begin, so we understand the vocabulary and cooking methods prior to entering the kitchen. It takes only a little time for us to get into a routine. But, it takes a lifetime to understand the Italian language and the skills of listening, spelling, and handling money to become in sync with the Italian people.

The place setting has three forks and one knife. The fork for salad and the entreé are to the left and a single knife to the right, the dessert fork is at the top. There are two glasses per setting, one for water and one for wine.

INTENSIVE COURSE IN REGIONAL CUISINE

The principal's letter

The Marco Polo Foundation of Lecce in conjunction with IPSSART (the State sponsored professional training school for Hotel and Hospitality Service as well as Restaurants and Tourism) located in the city of Otranto have designed an Intensive Course based on a set of protocols and standards for American Culinary students coming from Monroe College in New York City since 2004. This intensive course in the ancient arts of healthy cooking and attractive/elaborate table presentations, in the point of view of this office will be considered a permanent imprint and the training as "life-long learning." IPSSART will be training a group of students from Monroe College who have crossed the Atlantic with expectations and different dreams to learn Mediterranean Regional Cuisine in the first city of their 3 month journey. Salento, the region to the South of Apulia which faces the Mediterranean Sea is known for its ancient farming traditions and its natural resources (plants, soil, and climate). Agriculture has shaped the community in its production of typical foods that are good to eat and has enhanced the gastronomical activities that make up daily life. A request by consumers for a healthy diet and a healthy dietary regime that incorporates both typical and antique flavors had urged the local farm worker and not just him, in some part- a sector of the restaurant industry to rediscover these typical products and through traditional culinary methods to connect them.

For these students new to Mediterranean way-of-life given that state-of-the-arts kitchen facilities are at their disposal and regular scheduled cooking classes followed by a banquet of their prepared dishes, both eating customs and the foods will be a sensory overload of smells, tastes and flavor, colors and composition, and understanding how certain organoleptic flavor profiles develop from the cooking techniques learned. For some, Mediterranean living has created a new digestive habit and in some ways overcome the awaited for extreme intrusiveness of the stereotypical cooking originating in mass marketed, mass produced foods of an industrialized origin. In an attempt to facilitate the communication between English speaking students and Italian speaking teachers a few English translators work closely with the chef and administrators building the relationship of different cultures and to implement a new cultural syncretism which suggests the capacity for a common value system and ideals. The daily scheduled cooking *classes became an encounter with the people of the Adriatic and also the Mediterranean people to them.*

The flavors of Puglian cuisine were disseminated to the students in increments, in an orderly way to introduce unlikely pairings of unfamiliar ingredients and in a way to begin building upon a repertoire of somewhat recognizable recipes which the students may have an established affinity for already. The collection of recipes discussed before each lesson were referred to as "gastronomic deposits" that bring pleasure to the table in a discovery of the rich, artistic heritage and for the cultural traditions in Puglia, a territory known throughout Italy for its seaside resorts vacationland.

Meanwhile, at the Chamber of Commerce next to the packages that advertise the ecological wonders and architectural landmarks of Puglia were a different set of offerings including thematic excursions called "the streets of oil and wine" through the Salentine countryside between farms, olive groves, crushers, vineyards and wineries. These would be roads and by-ways linking the farm to the processing facilities and the small villages that support an agricultural based lifestyle. On the other hand as far as cooking is concerned, is that oil and wine are to be considered the most important ingredients of this cuisine linking pasta to the other nutritional components of a Mediterranean diet and for the development of agriculture in Puglia, and the Salentine. The wine sector contributes significantly to meal planning as it is included in daily life gastronomics, wine with the daily meals is as common place as the boasting by companies in Puglia who have consolidated their efforts to bring Puglian wine making to an international level. A food cooperative of 350 farms all bring their grapes to a central processing plant that measures each load of grapes for sugar content and grades them by this quality for the wines they make scientifically selected for sophistication. Students will have the opportunity to tour this wine making cooperative and see first-hand the technological skills involved in this undertaking.

Also within the realm of possibilities for growing the food which is to eat, are problems relating to the safeguarding of parent strains of certain plants by genetic typing, the ones supported by the indigenous ecosystem. This allows the local population to rely on a constant supply of a certain quality produce grown in the agrosphere. The Italians have been monitoring genetic profiles of some species, especially grapes and olives and then study the dispersal of these strains across their country and other continents in order to validate original parental strains or identify same varieties given different names long after transplantation. In an attempt to continue accurate identification of these plants and provide protection to certain varieties that really only grow in a select region, the Italian government has created a system of protection/identification of place of origin for Italian produce and certain Italian products. Students will learn more about IDP and IGP as they are introduced to the various indigenous foods of Italian origin.

The Marco Polo Project has made provision for acquisition of specific skills that take into consideration following the trail of raw food ingredients from point of purchase

since they first made an appearance on the day's menu until the moment that they arrive "closely guarded" on the table for service. This includes learning how to negotiate with merchants for their wares, and becoming intimately acquainted with a unique diversity of merchants who sell at open-air markets, farmer's markets, or specialty stores. Italian chefs are often required to select fresh local ingredients on any given day as they provide absolutely the freshest ingredients from market to table. They must also learn to critique the ingredients for the flavors they wish to offer in their prepared dishes. Knowledge of innovations in food conservation, seasoning and preparation of products will turn these students into catering operators who recognize what it takes to opt for quality catering. We wish the best of luck to our friends in their endeavors and on their culinary adventures and feel confident in their grasp of authentic Italian foods and the presentation of meals according to Italian traditions.

Recipients of our certification for the Intensive Course in Mediterranean Cuisine must be able to demonstrate their understanding of a basic skill set, and the methodologies required to skillfully handle them in a fashion appropriate to the undertaking of a career in typical restaurants. The students will have the opportunity to intern in several local restaurants during their time in the city of Otranto, and shadow the preparations of the chef from stove to table. Upon their return to the United States, students from Monroe College are encouraged to share their expertise gained in the many cultural areas of learning from Salento, a land full of charm, with their peers who might also be interested in a life-changing opportunity as the study of regional cuisines in Italy. Students will take with them stories about their favorite chefs and teachers, memories and impressions on the foods they ate, and a complete record of every recipe they tried while training at IPSSART culinary center. The collaboration of IPSSART of Otranto with the Marco Polo Foundation has enabled many students from the Monroe College in New York City to learn culinary techniques of the Salentine and Mediterranean. In contrast, by means of different training processes and the spirit of Hospitality, students will obtain a rapport with American food in order to achieve a healthy diet, consolidated by correct ancient principles that are still valid today.

Professor Bruno Constantino
Executive Director IPSSART Otranto

The "school building" is called an Edificio Scolastico, there is an accredited professional cooking school for hotels, restaurants and tourism located here as recognized by the Italian State. But we must wait until someone unlocks the front door and the chef arrives with the support staff before going inside.

Thanks for everything. From the school administrator to the English teacher who transformed our learning experience, the people of Otranto are the friendliest and most polite people on Earth. Hugs & kisses to everyone from the marco polo group 2009, nine students ready for a unique learning adventure. We sure had some fun.

Today's menu

Risotto gamberi e sprak-risotto with shrimp and bacon

First course- risotto

Dentice al forno con olive-Catch of the day baked whole in olive oil and lemon juice with green olives

Second course fish

Torta pasticiotto-pastry cream filled tart with top crust

Dolce-dessert

1) These Mediterranean fish are called Dentice because they have teeth. This is the Dentice out of the oven. We pan roasted them whole with lemons and olives plus a little water and wine

2) Then, we picked the meat away from the bones serving the baked fish and the olives. 3) The dessert is a Torta Pasticiotto. A traditional pasta frolla crust filled with cooked pastry cream.-

Today's menu

Linguine agli scampi-Jumbo shrimps served with linguine and tomato, garlic sauce

First course pasta-linguine

Polpo in pignata-Octopus in a pot

Second course fish-octopus

Peperoni in agrodolce-sweet and sour bell peppers and onions

Contourno- vegetables

1) My first chance to cook an octopus and I am wearing a disposable mesh coat. The octopus is pulled from a pot of boiling water once it turns pink. 2) Linguine is plated with scampi shrimp. 3) The young student smiles after shrimps cooking in garlic sauce are flambeau in brandy.

Today's Menu

Pitta di patate-mashed potatoes baked with a crusty top

Antipasto-appetizer

Orrechiette alla Lecce-Ear shaped pasta in regional sauce

First course- pasta

Arrosto di carne-roasted meat

Second course-meat

Torta mimosa-pineapple and pastry cream in a baked tart

Dolce-dessert

Today's menu

Insalata di polpo-octopus and pickled vegetables in salad with tomatoes

Antipasto-octopus salad

Spaghetti alle cozze-popular dish with black mussels and spaghetti

First course-pasta

Filetto di spigola al cartoccio-Sea bass baked in foil

Second course-fish

Cipolle gratinate- au gratin onions

Contourno- vegetable dish

The octopus salad is composed of cooked octopus, the legs are scaled of the cups and cut into bite size pieces, mixed vegetables of carrot, celery, and broccoli are blanched and pickled in vinaigrette assembled on salad greens and tomatoes.

Today's menu

We are in luck today someone showed up with 3 lbs of mystery meat.

Agnolotti alla piemontese-Fresh cut round pasta filled with ground veal and diced vegetables

First course pasta-fresh agnolotti

Pezzetti di cavallo-pieces of horsemeat

Second course meat

Peperonata alle olive nere-pan roasted peppers with black olives

Contourno-vegetable dish

Today's menu

A special occasion menu

Bruschette-brush olive oil on sliced bread bake a few minutes, rub a garlic clove on one side of hot toasted bread, top with small diced tomato salsa with salt, lemon juice, parsley or basil

Pureed fava beans with chicory- a wild salad with dip

Small risotto dish with bacon, arugula and perfume of forest

Filet beef according to maitre d'hotel

Cooked spinach with pine nuts & raisins

Nut brown potatoes-a melon baller is used to make small rounds

Fruit layered crostata-pastry cream filled shell and seasonal fruit glossed with jam

Our culinary group sat twelve at the dinner table, although at our
special occasion we put in a second long table and asked twelve guests
to join us, plus four local students to lend a hand in the kitchen.

1) This is a classic risotto dish with bacon, arugula, and mushrooms. 2) We started the meal with a simple salad of mixed greens, the radicchio makes for a bitter salad.

ITALIAN COOKING VOCABULARY

Puglia region

Acciughe-anchovy
Aceto di vino bianco-white wine vinegar
Acqua-water
Acqua naturale-bottled water
Acqua frizzante-effervescent bottled water
Aglio-garlic
Albiocche-apricot
Alloro-Bay leaf, aka laurel leaf
Anguilla-eel
Aragosta-lobster
Arancini-rice balls, deep fried shaped as oranges
Arrabbiata- angry, hot from red chili flakes
Axenthio- Absinthe
Balsamico-balsamic vinegar
Basilica-basil
Brodo-broth
Bruschette-crispy bread with topping /appetizer
Bucatini-thick tube pasta
Burro-butter
Caffe-expresso
Caffe Americano- expresso thinned with extra hot water
Calamari-deep fried squid rings
Capperi-capers
Carciofi-artichokes
Carne-meat
Carote-carrot
Carpaccio-meat or fish appetizer/served as very thin slices
Cavatappi-spiral macaroni
Cibo-food
Cipolle-onion

Cipollini-small onions
Cocomero-watermelon
Conchiglie- sea shell pasta
Cornetto- croissant
Cotto- ricotta cheese
Cozze-mussels
Cuccichiaio-spoon, spoonful
Cuocere- to cook
Cuoco-the cook
Datteri-dates
Dentice-Sea bream
Farfalle-bow tie shaped pasta
Farina-flour
Fichi-figs
Fiore-flower
Foglia-leaf
Foglio-sheet, (paper or foil)
Fontina-favorite semi-hard cheese
Forchetta- a fork
Formaggio-cheese
Formaggio fresco piccante-pressed cottage cheese with red hot chili pepper flakes
Forte-strong
Fragole-strawberry
Fresco-fresh
Funghi-mushrooms
Fusilli-spirals pasta
Gamberi-prawns
Gamberetti- shrimps
Gamberoni-big shrimps
Gelato-fresh rich ice cream
Gnocchis-small potato dumplings
Gorgonzola-blue cheese
Grana- finely grated parmesan cheese
Grana padano- parmiggiano reggiano graded as seconds, used for grating
Granita-fruit slushy
Grappa- distilled grape spirits
Grata-grated parmesan cheese, shaved or shredded
Lasagna-flat sheet pasta
Latte-milk
Lattuga-lettuce

Lessare-to boil

Lievito-yeast, fresh brewer's yeast

Limone-lemon

Linguine-fatter than spaghetti

Macedonia- light refreshing fruit salad

Manzo-beef

Melagrana-pomegranate

Melanzone-eggplant

Mele-apple

Melone-melon

Miele-honey

Misto-mixed, a variety

Moscardini-little octopuses

Noce moscara-nutmeg

Olio d'oliva-olive oil

Orecchiette- pasta shaped like little ears

Origano-oregano

Padre Piu-the newest saint, from Puglia region

Pane-bread

Panna-cream

Panna Montana-whipped cream

Pannocotta-a dessert, molded cooked cream with syrup topping

Parmiggiano reggiano- first rate aged parmesan cheese

Patate-potato

Pecorino romano-a favorite hard cheese made in Puglia region

Pepe-pepper

Peperone-bell pepper

Peperoncino-hot peppers

Pere-pear

Pesca-peach

Pesca noce-nectarine

Pesce-fish

Pesce spada- swordfish

Piatto- plate

Piselli- peas

Pollo- chicken

Polpo- octopus

Pomodoro-tomato

Pomodori pelati-peeled tomatoes

Pompelmo-grapefruit

Porcini- mushroom from northern Italy
Prezzemelo- parsley
Proscuitto- cured & dried ham, generally sliced paper thin
Prugne-prune plums
Radicchio- a red lettuce, somewhat bitter
Raffreddare-to cool down
Ragu- browned meat and tomato cooked into sauce
Riso-rice
Risotto- a favorite slow-cooked rice mainstay
Ricotta forte- a strong pungent form of ricotta
Rosmarino- rosemary
Rucola- arugula
Sale-salt
Salmone- salmon
Salsa- sauce
Salvataggio-your lifeguard
Salvia- sage
Sarde- sardines
Schiacciare-mashed
Scampi-a dish made with prawns
Scorsa di limone- grated lemon peel
Sedano- celery
Semolina- yellow wheat flour used for making fresh pasta
Seppia- cuttlefish
Speak- lean italian bacon, also called sprak
Stampo-a pastry mold
Tonno- tuna
Tuorli- egg yolks
Uova- eggs
Uva- grapes
Uvetta- raisins
Vagnilia- vanilla
Verdura- green groceries
Vino blanco-white wine
Vino rosso- red wine
Vitello- veal
Vognoles- clams, a type of Japanese clam being cultivated in Mediterranean
Zucchero-sugar
Zucchine-zucchini
Zuppe Inglese-trifle

The exuberant chef demonstrates butchering techniques on a veal shoulder. We are going to brown the veal scallops and slow cook them in tomato sauce with peas.

THE RECIPES-MEDITERRANEAN CUISINE

Antipasti

Primi-first course

Seconde di pesce- second course fish

Seconde di carne-second course meat

Contourni-vegetables

Dolce-dessert

The waitress carries swordfish & shrimps from the kitchen to the front dining room.

ANTIPASTI

Food served at the beginning of an Italian meal; a light dish, salad, soup, or appetizer

ARANCINI

Little Oranges, deep fried stuffed rice balls

Serves 10

Ingredients

Arborio rice	1 lb
Onion, minced	2 oz
Meat broth	1 ¾ pints
Butter	3 ½ oz
White wine	2 fl oz
Fontina cheese	7 oz
Proscuitto, mince cut	5 oz
Whole eggs	2 each
Breadcrumbs	as much as needed
Parmesan cheese, grated	as much as needed
Salt & Pepper	as much as needed
Saffron	as much as needed

Preparation

➤ Toast the rice in a sauté pan with melted butter and onion.

➤ Bathe the rice with white wine and let it evaporate. Add the saffron.

➤ Bathe the rice with meat broth. Add the broth a little bit at a time until it obtains a consistency very much al dente.

➤ Pull from the heat and unite the rice mixture with the fontina cut into cubes, the grated cheese and the prosciutto mince cut.

➢ Make it cool down in the refrigerator. When you are ready add the eggs, correct the seasoning for salt & pepper and bring it all together.

➢ Form the little oranges in the palms of your hands, roll them into the breadcrumbs. Deep fry in an abundance of oil for 2-3 minutes a few at a time.

BRUSCHETTE

Crispy bread with tomato topping

Serves 10

Ingredients

Fresh baguettes, sliced	3 lbs
Red tomatoes	1 lb
Olive oil	5 fl oz
Salt & Oregano	as much as needed
Garlic cloves	2 each

Preparation

➢ Brush oil onto both sides of the sliced bread. Place on a baking pan and slide into the oven heated to 350' F. Flip the slices during cooking and remove from the oven when golden. Allow about 10 minutes all together until done.

➢ Crush a garlic clove right into the hot crispy bread over one side.

➢ Prepare a medium dice of the fresh tomatoes and spice with salt & oregano, a dash more olive oil to stir, and chopped parsley to finish.

Variations according to regional preferences:

1. Add arugula and bacon

2. Add mushrooms and olive paté

3. Add baby eels and chili peppers

4. Add boiled vegetables, pinyon pine nuts and olive slices

CARPACCIO DI SALMONE

Salmon carpaccio

Serves 10

Ingredients

Fresh salmon	1 lb
Lemon juice	as much as needed
Olive oil	as much as needed
Salt & Pepper	as much as needed

Preparation

➢ To filet the salmon begin with frozen, and slice off layers that are like little envelopes or which could be rolled up.

➢ Remove the slices, layer at a time.

➢ Prepare a marinade of the rest of the ingredients, and pour over the sliced salmon cuts systematically in a heat-resistant dish.

➢ Leave in infusion for at least 2 hours, drain and serve.

COCKTAIL DI GAMBERETTI

Shrimp cocktail

Serves 10

Ingredients

Shelled shrimp	2 lbs
mayonnaise	1 lb
Ketchup	as much as needed
Worcester sauce	as much as needed
Brandy	as much as needed
Radicchio	as much as needed
Salad greens	as much as needed
Heavy cream	3 ½ fl oz
Lemon juice	as much as needed

Preparation

Place a shallow pan of water on the stove, adding the juice of one half a lemon. Bring to a boil and cook the shrimps for about 5 minutes. Drain and let cool. In a serving tureen put the mayonnaise and incorporate the heavy cream, the ketchup, the Worcester sauce and the brandy. Stir it all up to obtain a smooth, homogenous composition. Wash the radicchio and salad greens, dry and put them together to dress 10 salad plates. Toss the shrimps into the cocktail sauce and systematically coat them with a thin veil, build the shrimp cocktail according to your taste and serve.

IMPASTO PER PIZZA NAPOLETANA

Dough for pizza of Naples

Serves 10

Ingredients

Semolina flour	1 3/8 lb
Olive oil	2 ½ oz
Instant yeast	1 oz
Water, salt	as much as needed

Preparation

➤ Systematically on your work surface take the flour and mound it like a fountain, add the oil, the yeast and with nimble fingers work in tepid water and a pinch of salt; amalgamate everything, working the dough well and leave it to rise covered for 3-4 hours.

➤ **Pizza margherita:** (named for Italian queen) peeled tomatoes, mozzarella, green olives, olive oil, oregano

➤ **Pizza napoletana:** (Naples style) peeled tomatoes, mozzarella, anchovies, capers, olive oil, oregano

➤ **Pizza capricciosa:** (capricious) peeled tomatoes, mozzarella, chopped prosciutto, mushrooms, artichokes, oregano, capers, green olives, olive oil

➤ **Pizza primavera:** (spring) fresh ripe tomatoes, mozzarella, chipped parmesan cheese, arugula, olive oil

INSALATA DI POLPO

Octopus salad

Serves 10

Ingredients

Octopus, fresh	4 lbs
Celery, julienne	10 oz
Carrot, julienne	10 oz
Parsley, minced	as much as needed
Olive oil	as much as needed
Salt, pepper	as much as needed
Lemon juice	as much as needed
Salad tomatoes - cut	10 oz

Preparation

➢ Boil the octopus until just done, clean the octopus by removing the oculus, and cut the octopus into bite-size pieces.

➢ Season the octopus with the olive oil, salt & pepper, and lemon juice.

➢ Add the cut vegetables and mix the two together.

➢ Dust with parsley and serve cold.

MISTO DI MARE

Seafood salad plate

Lettuce julienne

Arugula

Octopus, cooked and large dice

Arancini, 1 or 2 deep fried rice balls

Fish fillet, small floured and deep fried

Mussels, 4 steamed open

Tomato, small dice to top the steamed mussels

Mussels, 2 steamed open and covered in bread crumbs

Pickled sardines, 3

Lemon wedge

Preparations

Assemble the plate with a bed or lettuce and arugula, the mussels must be cooked until open and topped, the fillet should be a major component, the cooked octopus second component, arancini as a centerpiece, sardines at the finish. Serve with a lemon wedge.

Prepare the arancini in advance and cook them before the fillets. Allow to cool to room temperature and assemble warm. Cut the octopus into pieces after boil and out of the cooking pot.

PARMIGIANA DI MELANZANE

Eggplant Parmesan

Serves 10

Ingredients

Eggplants	4 lbs
Tomato sauce	3 ½ fl oz
Olive oil	7 fl oz
Oil for frying	as much as needed
Flour	1 lb
Whole eggs	10 each
Salt	a little
Water	enough for a batter
Cheese, lightly grated	7 oz

Preparation

➢ Prepare a batter with eggs, flour, water, and salt.

➢ Cut the eggplants in slices, drop them in the batter and fry them in the frying oil.

➢ Build the dish in a casserole, systematically alternating layers of the eggplants, then tomato sauce and cheese.

➢ Put in the oven at 350'F until done, when the surface turns golden.

PITTA DI PATATE

Double crusted potatoes

Serves 10

Ingredients

Potatoes, boiled	3 lbs
Green olives	per your taste
Olive oil	7 fl oz
Whole eggs	3 each
Proscuitto, chopped	7 oz
Anchovies, soaked in oil	per your taste
Parmesan cheese, grated	5 oz
Salt & Pepper	as much as needed
Parsley, minced	as much as needed
Tomato sauce	3 ½ oz
Onions to stretch recipe	1 lb

Preparation

➤ Boil the potatoes. Let them chill down before mashing.

➤ Throw the onions into the pan, cover in oil and sauté until translucent, then add all these ingredients; chopped prosciutto, minced anchovies, salt & pepper, tomato sauce and parsley.

➤ Stir these ingredients into the onions to form a mixture, and cook 2-3 minutes on a low heat. Remove from heat and blend into the mashed potatoes.

➤ Grease a baking dish with oil, pour in the mixture. Finally, beat the eggs slightly and pour over the potatoes. Fold the eggs lightly into the surface, turning over to incorporate, then dust the surface with all the grated cheese and put into an oven heated to 400' F.

➢ Take out of the oven when the surface has turned golden. Allow to cool down before serving.

PURE'DI FAVE CON CICORIE SELVATICHE

Spread of puree fava beans with wild chicory

Serves 10

Ingredients

Wild chicory	4 lbs
Dried fava, without shell	2 lbs
Extra virgin olive oil	4 1/3 fl oz
Butter	as much as needed
Sliced baguette	as much as needed
Salt	as much as needed

Preparation

➤ In a large sauté pan to cook the fava, with enough water to cover them, for about 1 hour letting them boil slowly. After an hour add the salt and with a wooden ladle mash and stir continuously to the finish when obtaining a homogenous puree. (The fava should be cooked until soft enough to mash. The cooking water can be almost expired or added to the puree).

➤ Then take from the heat and add 3 1/2 fl oz of extra virgin olive oil.

➤ Now in another sauté pan bring to a boil enough water necessary to boil the chicory. (The leaves can be large enough to top a crostini when served, or chopped into somewhat smaller pieces).

➤ Meanwhile, heat up a bit of butter in a fry pan and fry the baguette crostini.

➢ Once cooked, to prevent stickiness, season the chicory with the remaining olive oil.

➢ You spill out the fava and the chicory in the same plate and serve together alongside fried crostini which are prepared.

VEGETABLE PIE

I asked Maria for a recipe with olives because I believed olives would be a popular ingredient in Mediterranean cuisine. She remarked that she really didn't care for olives but offered two dishes that were commonly prepared with olives. This one is called vegetable pie.

Ingredients

Onion	1 large
Garlic	2 cloves
Salt & pepper	to taste
Spices	hot, oregano
Zucchini	1 lb, sliced
Eggplant	1 lb, cut into pieces
Pitted black olives	1 can, drained, chopped
Ripe red tomatoes	1 lb fresh, chopped
Tomato paste	4 oz paste
Tomato sauce	14 oz sauce
Canned tuna	1 can, drained
Lasagna noodles	1 box
Pecorino cheese	4 oz, cubes
Parmesan cheese	4 oz, grated
Bread crumbs	6 oz crumbs

Procedure

The vegetable pie will be cooked in a baking dish for lasagna at 350'F for 35 minutes or until the top crust is done. Assemble in a couple steps. If the lasagna noodles need to be cooked first, prepare them in advance and let them cool down in cold water. Heat the tomato sauce and tomato paste, leave on the stove top at lowest temperature. In a fry pan, pour in some oil and start to cook the garlic, the onion and the zucchini. To make the pie easier to assemble take the warm vegetables off the heat and allow them to cool at room temperature to the side in a bowl. In the same fry pan, heat the eggplant with some olive and turn until browned, add the fresh tomatoes and black olives. Set them to the side and prepare the baking pan for assembly. Add the salt & pepper to the vegetables, the oregano to the eggplants and fresh tomatoes, if you are using hot spice add that to the cooked tomato sauce. Oil the pan and set a bottom layer of lasagna noodles in the pan. Spoon in some sauce and vegetables, layer the eggplants and tomatoes then cover with another layer of noodles and sauce. In the next layer, sauce, and spread the tuna into the vegetables cover with lasagna noodles. The next layer spoon sauce, remaining vegetables and fontina cheese cubes. Cover with top layer and any sauce, the parmesan cheese and bread crumbs. Cover with foil and bake 35-45 minutes. The last ten minutes, check to see if the top has a golden crust and remove the foil. Take from oven when done.

ZUPPE DI COZZE CON CROSTINI

Black mussels in broth with toasts

Serves 10

Ingredients

Black mussels	5 lbs
Fresh baguette	2 lbs
Olive oil	7 fl oz
Chopped garlic	2 cloves
Pepper	as much as needed
Parsley, minced	as much as needed
Tomato sauce	3 ½ oz

Preparation

➤ Clean the mussels and wash them well.

➤ Heat the oil and garlic, cooking until the garlic is browned.

➤ Add the mussels to the cooking pan and stir them over a high heat until all the shells have opened up. Reduce the heat and cover the mussels with just enough water. Simmer.

➤ Heat either canned or fresh tomatoes in a sauce pan, when hot remove from heat and puree using an immersion blender, strain through a food mill. The tomato sauce can now be added to the mussels in broth, also toss in the minced parsley.

➤ Serve with the bread that has previously been toasted in the oven.

PRIMI

These dishes are called the first course; they are most often pasta or rice courses.

The husband and wife are happy owners of a restaurant in Southern Italy, he is the chief cook.

AGNOLETTI ALLA PIEMONTESE

Fresh pasta Piedmont style

Serves 10

Ingredients

Fresh pasta, made with eggs	22 oz
Veal shoulder	18 oz
Mirepoix	5 oz
Olive oil	3 ½ fl oz
Parmesan cheese	5 oz
Nutmeg	as much as needed
Butter	3 ½ oz
White wine	2 fl oz
Whole eggs	3 each
Sage leaves	as many as needed

*mirepoix is a mix of aromatic vegetables usually celery, carrot, and onion in a 1:1:1 ratio, which are finely chopped and added to improve nutritional value, and aroma to a main course.

Preparation

➢ Take a large sauté pan and pour in the oil, lightly brown the mirepoix.

➢ Unite with it the meat cut into pieces and continue cooking over a high heat.

➢ (The remainder of the veal shoulder can be tossed into a stock pot of water to make meat broth; a few vegetables should do to give the broth ample flavoring. Cook the meat broth on a rolling boil until needed then lower heat).

➢ Bathe the meat and mirepoix with the white wine, allow it to evaporate and cover with meat broth.

➢ When it has cooked down completely dry, pass it through a grinder a few times. Knead an egg or two into the mixture, the grated cheese and some nutmeg. Season with salt & pepper.

➢ You require 1 lb 6 oz fresh pasta for this recipe. Begin with 1 lb of semolina flour and 6 eggs. On a dry surface dusted with flour, make a mound of flour with a well in the center, whisk the eggs together and stir in the flour adding a little water if necessary. Work it into a dough and let the dough chill in the refrigerator for 1 hour before rolling it out.

➢ Take the fresh pasta dough and roll it into thin sheets of a thickness 1.5 mm in shapes of lasagna. Trim off the ends and lay flat to dry sprinkled with a little flour.

➢ Use the egg wash on one sheet of pasta ribbon, while at regular distances set some meat filling, cover with the pasta that has not been brushed with egg wash.

➢ Seal and cut in round forms. Boil in salted water. Melt 3 ½ oz butter and flavor with fresh sage leaves. Remove agnoletti from the pot and toss them in butter with sage. To serve sprinkle with grated parmesan or pecorino cheese.

BUCATINI ALL'AMATRICIANA

Bucatini in a connaisseur's sauce

Serves 10

Ingredients

Bucatini pasta	2 lbs
Guanciale or Pancetta	7 oz
Onions	2 each
Garlic	1 clove
Peeled Tomatoes	4 lbs
Pecorino cheese	2 oz
Hot peppers	as much as needed
Olive oil	2 oz
Salt & Parsley	as much as needed
Bread crumbs	7 0z
Grated Parmesan cheese	7 oz

Preparation

➢ Cut into small dice the Guanciale or Pancetta by rolling it up first, then dice and step up to cook in a skillet with olive oil, the onions minced also the garlic clove minced. Saute until golden and unite in the skillet your tomatoes, cut up into small pieces. Salt the tomatoes now cooking in the skillet, after you are well into cooking the sauce for a few minutes first, take it away from the fire adding the hot peppers. To thicken the sauce, add 7 oz bread crumbs, and another 7 oz grated parmesan cheese. Make to cook the bucatini in salted water; drain them when al dente, flavor with the sauce prepared and with the parsley and the grated pecorino cheese.

CICERI E TRIA

Chickpeas in a triad of noodles and crispy wontons

*This is a dish usually served in the winter, although it has a special place to be made for Father's Day. Called St. Joseph's Day in Italy traditionally the dish is passed to the poor on the occasion of "bowl day."

Serves 10

Ingredients

Chickpeas	1 lb
Flour	1 2/3 lbs
Olive oil	5 oz
Water, salt & pepper	as much as needed
Celery	3 ½ oz
Carrot	3 ½ oz
Onion	5 oz
Tomato	5 oz

Preparation

➤ Soak the chick peas in water and salt the night before; the next morning rinse them thoroughly and systematically put them in a pressure cooker with water, cooking them over low flame.

➤ When the chickpeas are softened drain the water and combine with the aromatic vegetables (celery, carrot, onion, and tomato) that have been chopped to a small dice. Stir together for a uniform mixture and cover all these elements with a minimum amount of water. Return to a boil and cook vegetables on low. Turn off heat and allow to rest at room temperature. Do not drain away this liquid. It is reserved to provide the final dish with a modicum of broth.

➢ On a flat floured surface prepare a pasta dough with flour from grain, water and salt; stretch it out and to flatten with a rolling pin forming a sheet with a thickness of one millimeter.

➢ Roll out the sheet and with a knife trim away the uneven edges leaving a rectangular shape. Cut this into three pieces about 10 cm in length.

➢ Systematically put the three in a tray dusted with flour and hang them to dry sheltered from air currents.

➢ Take one third and cut into small pieces for frying. Use the quantity of oil necessary to flavor the pasta and chickpeas. Heat the oil to sizzling and fry the harvested pasta third until they plump and become well defined. This can be done in batches. Scoop from the hot oil and arrange on a baking sheet, place in the oven until they crisp up. Smaller lengths and thinner cuts will get hard as soon as they begin to darken, do not over-cook this share of the pasta, they should be considered as wontons. Use a low oven heat and be careful not to burn.

➢ The remaining two-thirds share should be passed through a pasta machine for even cuts of the entire length. Place these cuts on tray and dust with flour.

➢ Put a share of the pasta about 5 oz into boiling water until al dente. Scoop out and cool in a cold water bath. Boil the remainder in this way until very much al dente.

➢ Remove wontons from oven. Now you have the three components.

➢ Unite them in the frying oil, coat the cooked pasta first, then chickpeas with aromatic vegetables in broth, and third the wontons. Amalgamate them all, mixing and serve right away after you sprinkle with a bit of pepper.

➢ Cooked pasta is generally coated with oil after boiling because the olive oil is part of the diet. Toss the pasta in hot oil, add the chick peas and coat them, too. Fill the bowls with pasta and chick peas and top off with broth, the crispy pasta is a final garnish. Add cracked pepper if you like.

This is one of those recipes that require you to have a pasta roller. If you don't have the pasta rolling machine substitute rigatoni for the dry pasta, and look in your dairy aisle for fresh pasta that can be used in this way to fry up crispy and a fast bake to darken. We tried wonton wrappers with some success.

CICIERI E TRIA-RESTAURANT STYLE

Signature dish soup

One serving in large bowl, prepared in a small sauté over high flame

Ingredients

Ceci beans	3 oz
Olive oil	4 Tbsp
Onion	1 oz
Fresh pasta	8 oz
Fried pasta	2 oz
Cinnamon	½ tsp
Pepper	¼ tsp
Oregano	a pinch

*The cook used fresh pasta made that morning and bought from a small shop down the way. Since the pasta was somewhat curly, I call the wontons 'fried curly noodles'. He gave them a coat of olive oil, slipped them in the oven on a baking pan at medium heat until browned.

Preparation

➤ Heat oil in a small sauté pan, add onions. When they become translucent, add some ceci beans, about 3 oz. Toss the ingredients in the sauté pan a bit, the cooking of the ceci beans will add starch to the solution and thicken into gravy.

➤ Drop some fresh curly pasta into a water bath, when al dente add one cup for your portion to serve one bowlful to the sauté pan with the ceci beans. The already softened pasta will continue to cook and achieve a similar temperature as the ceci beans; some pasta water from cooking is desired for a broth. Continue to toss in order to combine or stir.

➢ Sprinkle cinnamon into the pan and add fried curly noodles that you have made previously. A little pepper is necessary. This should be about right. Take enough for one bowlful and garnish with fresh dried oregano across top in a linear pattern.

➢ Making this at home, I might add chopped celery, carrots, and tomatoes for color.

FARFALLE CARBONARA

Bowties pasta carbonara

Ingredients

Dry pasta bowties- 1 box

Smoked bacon-chopped raw, 2 oz per serving

Eggs-1 per serving, one extra

Milk-a couple ounces

Grated parmesan cheese- a couple ounces

Shaved parmesan-a couple ounces

Salt-pinch

Red hot chili pepper flakes-pinch

Preparations

Farfalle pasta is commonly known as bowties, and you can find them at your grocery under either name. Begin by boiling water and adding some salt put in the bowties pasta enough for each person. Cook to al dente.

Use a small bowl to make the carbonara sauce. First separate the egg yolks from egg white. The egg yolks are counted one per serving, take a measuring spoon and add one Tbsp milk or cream to the egg yolks, measure one Tbsp parmesan cheese per serving into the yolks and cream. Stir it all up, add a pinch of salt. I also add one extra yolk to ensure the color of the coating to be extra yellow.

In a large fry pan cook the bacon, until almost done and pour off grease. Or use pancetta it will crisp up without much grease. Pour olive oil into the fry pan; enough to coat the bowties. Reheat the bacon in oil with chili flakes as soon as the pasta is cooked. Drain the pasta except for a spoonful of water and pour the pasta into the warm/hot oil. Once the oil is hot, the water will sizzle to evaporate. Stir with a wooden spoon. The bowties will shine with oil. Now you can add the carbonara sauce.

Pour the egg yolk mixture over the top and stir the pasta up from the bottom of the pan, getting all the pasta coated with carbonara, watch for the egg to cook and stick to the bottom of the pan, so be fast to stir the egg over the pasta so it coats the noodles instead of the pan. You will know it is done when the egg no longer looks fluid rather it has dried and sticks to the pasta.

Take off the heat and portion one plateful at a time. The carbonara will have bacon in parts throughout, and some chili flakes. Use your good parmesan cheese, shaved or flakes and toss a Tbsp full over the plate. Serve hot.

GNOCCHI DI PATATE AL GORGONZOLA

Gnocchi in a creamy gorgonzola sauce

Serves 10

Ingredients

Boiling Potatoes	4 lbs
Flour	1 lb
Gorgonzola cheese	½ lb
Grated Parmesan cheese	5 oz
Butter	5 oz
Heavy cream	1 pint
Salt & Pepper	as much as needed
Parsley, minced	as much as needed
Tomato sauce	1 quart

Preparation

➢ Boil the potatoes with the skin, scarcely ready to do- peel them and pass them in a potato ricer.

➢ Make to cool down the mashed potatoes and knead it with the flour/ add to it salt and pepper.

➢ To form gnocchi begin kneading until you obtain first a cylindrical shape, then by touch slice equal dimensions.

➢ Pass the pieces of gnocchi pasta dough off the ribs of a fork, squishing nimbly with the thumb.

➢ Prepare the sauce judging at face value, melt the butter in a saute pan and add then the gorgonzola and heavy cream.

➢ Heat the tomato sauce to a boil and allow the gnocchis to cook thoroughly in the tomato sauce.

➢ Make to boil all the sauce ingredients for a few minutes, toss into boiling sauce the gnocchi and saute them/flipping the gnocchi in sauce for coating, adding finally the crumbs of parmesan cheese and minced parsley. Remove from heat and serve.

➢ We used a tomato sauce to cook the gnocchis and spooned some buttery gorgonzola sauce over the plate finishing with parmesan cheese and parsley. The chef originally intended for us to cook up the gnocchis in the butter and gorgonzola cream sauce so ours was red and white.

LASAGNE ALLA BOLOGNESE

Lasagna classic Italian style

Serves 10

For the pasta

Flour	3 lbs
Whole eggs	12
Water	as much as needed
Parmesan cheese, crumbs	7 oz
Mozzarella	3 lbs

Sauce Bolognese

Lean fresh beef	1 lb
Butter	2 oz
Dried mushrooms	3 ½ oz
Olive oil	2 fl oz
Red wine	3 ½ fl oz
Onion	1 each
Carrot	1 each
Celery	2 oz
Tomato paste	5 oz
Flour	1 Tbsp
Peeled tomatoes	2 lbs
Broth	1 quart, 2 fl oz
Salt & Pepper	as much as needed
Garlic	1 clove

Bechamel sauce

Half and half	1 quart, 2 fl oz
Butter	3 oz
Flour	2 ½ oz

Preparation

> To make the pasta:

> Mix the flour with the eggs and a bit of water. Let the dough rest in the refrigerator for 1 hour.

> Pass the dough through a mechanical pasta roller and stretch out into a thin layer. Trim the pasta to the desired lengths and let dry at room temperature sprinkled with some flour.

> To make the Bolognese sauce:

> Mince the carrot, the onion, the celery and one clove of garlic finely and the mushroom which previously has been rehydrated in a bath. Put them all in a fry pan and leave to sizzle until browned with the oil and butter. Add the meat and leave it until browned, bathe with red wine and allow the wine to evaporate. Add the tomato paste and sprinkle with flour. Add the peeled tomatoes which have been heated to a boil and passed through a sieve to remove the seeds; stretch out with broth and make to cook on low for 45 minutes. Salt & pepper as much as needed.

> To make the Bechamel Sauce: Make a roux with butter and flour heated then bathe with warmed milk/or half and half mixed with a whisk until the sauce boils for 5 minutes. Add the nutmeg and salt as much as needed.

> Cook the pasta in salted water and then chill the noodles down. Fetch a baking tin and grease it with butter and spread out a layer of thin pasta. Flavor with the Bolognese sauce and with the Bechamel sauce, sprinkle with some parmesan cheese crumbs and grated mozzarella. Cover with another layer of thin pasta in an opposite direction and continue to cover as before. Make five layers and cover the top layer with Bolognese and béchamel. Sprinkle with the parmesan cheese crumbs and pinches of butter; finally put in the oven for 15 minutes at 325' F.

*The lasagna noodles have been cooked, the Bolognese sauce has been cooked, and the béchamel sauce. The lasagna casserole should be assembled while all ingredients are still warmed. The cooking time is short because you really only need melt the cheese and allow the ingredients to marry. To make the five-layer lasagna requires a deep dish, use a baking tin if possible.

LINGUINE AGLI SCAMPI

Linguine with Prawns

Serves 10

Ingredients

Prawns	1 lb 3 ½ oz
Oil	7 fl oz
Linguine pasta	1 lb 10 oz
Garlic	as much as needed
Parsley, minced	as much as needed
Tomato sauce	1 lb
Salt & Pepper	as much as needed
Brandy	as much as needed

Preparation

➤ Prepare a tomato sauce utilizing a deep pot with oil and garlic.

➤ Cut the prawns in half lengthwise and wash them.

➤ Make a well in a fry-pan with oil and garlic adding the crustaceans, parsley, the pepper, the salt and cook over a high heat for 5 minutes. Bathe them with brandy, making it to evaporate.

➤ Now, pour the tomato sauce over the prawns and cook again for several minutes.

➤ Boil the linguine, drain when al dente, toss the linguine with the scampi sauce and jump the scampi on top.

➤ Serve dusted with minced parsley.

MISTO RISO

Summery rice salad

Ingredients

Cooked rice	3 cups
Tuna	1 package albacaore
Arugula	1 cup fresh
Tomatoes	2 each, chopped
Carrot	2 each, shredded
Cocktail olives	2 oz, sliced
Marinated artichoke hearts	4 oz, diced
Salt	to taste
Olive oil	1/3 cup
White wine vinegar	1/3 cup
Broth	1 quart to cook the rice
Lemon juice	1 Tbsp
Parsley	1 Tbsp
Pepper	to taste
Mayonnaise	3 Tbsp

Preparation

This is a refreshing summer dish similar to our potato salad. After the rice is cooked, the other ingredients are chopped, sliced and shredded accordingly. Then they are added to the rice and folded in with a wooden spoon. To dress the salad are nearly equal parts olive oil and white wine vinegar, only a small amount of lemon juice, salt & oregano to taste, and broth to cook the rice in to add flavor. As a final component is fresh cracked pepper and chopped parsley, tossed with a minimum amount of mayonnaise to coat everything, and serve at once.

ORECCHIETTE ALLA LECCESE

Ear shaped pasta with flavors of Lecce

*As we made the orecchiette by hand, we were told that they are referred to as "little Pope's hats." The orecchiette pasta is now in your food aisle in the States. On the other hand, this strong ricotta is not available. It is like stirring a spoonful of horseradish into the tomato ragu. I have included a recipe for homemade ricotta forte cheese.

Serves 10

Ingredients

Semolina flour	1 lb 10 oz
Tomato sauce	1 pint 14 fl oz
Ground meat	7 oz
Ricotta forte	as much as needed
Basil leaves	as many as needed
Pecorino cheese	as much as needed

Preparation

➢ Make the semolina flour into a dough using water and starting on a flat surface make a well in the middle of the flour add some water and begin to combine. Form a length of cord from this pasta and then by touching slice into small lengths with a knife and extract from the pieces then the orecchiette. Take a small cylindrical shape and roll it into a ball, flatten it on the thumb, then turn it inside out. It should appear flat and semi rounded, now it just sits on the thumb like a cap. Toss the little hats onto a tray and sprinkle with some flour. Allow to dry before cooking.

➢ Make to dry the pasta, in parts prepare the sauce from the cooked tomatoes add to it browned ground meat, a little ricotta forte and the basil leaves. Take all of it to a boil for 5 minutes over a low heat.

➢ Put the orecchiette into salted boiling water and jump them out with the prepared sauce. Sprinkle at the end with Pecorino from Lecce and serve decorated with a leaf of basil.

RICOTTA FORTE

Strong ricotta

Ingredients

Heavy cream, separated	1 quart
Apple cider vinegar	1 fl oz
Salt	1 tsp

Bring to 200'F and pour into cheesecloth allowing the liquid to drip. When it has stopped dripping, skim off from the cheesecloth and chill. Use within one week.

Strong ricotta

Ingredients

Heavy cream, separated	2 quarts
Fresh whey, or powdered whey protein	1 quart
Milk	2 fl oz
Apple cider vinegar	2 fl oz
Salt	2 tsp

If you open the heavy cream, it will separate into curds & whey. Add whey protein powder to a quart of water and cook the curds & whey, add the milk and apple cider vinegar. Cook to 200'F, Pour into cheesecloth hanging over a deep pot or a colander, allowing the liquid to drip. When it has stopped dripping it is ready to scoop out and chill. Makes about 1 ½ cups.

PAGLIA E FIENO ALLA BOLOGNESE

Straw hats and hay Bolognese style

Ingredients

Semolina flour	2 lbs
Whole eggs	8 each
Cooked spinach	7 oz
Olive oil	7 fl oz
Ground beef	1 lb
Brunoise (celery, carrot, onion)	5 oz
Tomato paste	5 oz
Dried Porcini mushrooms	2 oz
Peeled tomatoes	3 lbs
Parmesan cheese, grated	7 oz
Dry red wine	3 ½ fl oz
Salt, Pepper, Nutmeg	as much as needed

Preparation

➢ Divide the flour and eggs to prepare 2 separate doughs (one white and one green). Spinach is used to color and add flavor to the green noodle.

➢ Obtain a tagliatelle (long noodle, 1 cm wide or less) with the pasta rolling machine and put the pasta in bunches on a tray, sprinkle with some flour and let dry.

➢ Soak the dried mushrooms in hot water until they are reconstituted.

➢ To prepare the Bolognese sauce, take a large sauté pan and in it put the oil and the brunoise vegetables (chopped extra fine), wait until they have browned and to add the spongy mushrooms, which you have wrung out and chopped.

➤ To unite the ground minced meat and brown on a high heat, bathe with the wine and allow the wine to evaporate.

➤ To unite the tomato paste and the peeled tomatoes, adjust the seasonings of salt & pepper and cook on a low heat for about one hour.

➤ Boil the pasta to al dente, drain off the water, and leap right into the sauce you have prepared, turn off the heat and add the parmesan cheese (grated to crumbs).

RISOTTINO CON SPEAK,RUCOLA
E PROFUMI DI BOSCO

Special Risotto with bacon, arugula, and aromas of the forest

Ingredients for 10 people

Arugula	3 ½ oz
Fresh Porcini mushrooms	1 lb 7 oz
Rice	2 lbs
Vegetable broth	3 ½ pints
White onion of average size	1 each
Dry white wine	1 cup
Parsley	as needed
Grated parmesan & pecorino	5 oz
Butter	1 knob
Speak	7 oz

*Sprak or Speak is an Italian specialty meat similar to bacon without the fat. It is a lean bacon product, and tastes like bacon as we know it.

Procedure

➢ After having prepared at least 2 quarts plus 1 cup broth. In a pot, better if non-stick, prepare a bottom layer of oil with a knob of butter that you will melt. (I might fry up the bacon ahead of time in the pan. Reserve the bacon until the end. Continue cooking in the pan beginning with onion).

➢ Unite on the bottom the onion minced fine and make browned with the mushrooms fresh porcini that have been cut into segments rather thin.

➢ You add the rice already and you make it toast for 3 to 4 minutes on medium high heat, being careful you unite the dry white wine on maximum heat to make evaporate. Once the wine has evaporated, switch off the heat and allow the rice a resting period of ten minutes.

➤ After the necessary time has passed, revive the flame to a medium heat and begin to cook adding a ladle of broth at a time, adjust the salt and swirl the pan round frequently as the broth goes in, swirl the pan around.

➤ Once the rice is completely cooked, unite the other ingredients timed to the last ladle of broth; the grated cheeses, the reserved bacon and the arugula, (mostly whole leaves allowed to wilt in the final moments of cooking). Prior to service, sprinkle with chopped parsley.

RISOTTO AI GAMBERI E LIMONE

Shrimp and lemon risotto

Ingredients

Rice for risotto	2 lbs
Prawns	1 lb 7 oz
Lemons	2 each
Fish broth	2 quarts 4 fl oz
Butter	3 ½ oz
Olive oil	3 Tbsp
Garlic	1 clove
White wine	3 ½ fl oz
Salt, pepper, parsley	as much as needed

Preparation

➢ In a large sauté pan put the oil and brown the minced garlic. Add the rice and toast it, bathe with the white wine and once evaporated pour in the fish broth and cook for about 15 minutes. (If you need to make your own fish stock, it is composed of: saved fish, fish bones, vegetable mirepoix, water, white wine and as much salt as you need).

➢ In the meanwhile wash and clean the shrimps cutting them in half lengthwise add them to the risotto. (By our standards these shrimps are quite big, like langoustines. Cutting through the shell makes them easier to devour). For purpose of cooking put the butter in and dust with parsley.

➢ Garnish with lemon zest before chopping up the lemons into wedges.

RISOTTO AI GAMBERI E SPEAK

Bacon and Shrimp Risotto

Serves 10

Ingredients

Rice for risotto	2 lbs
Prawns	3 lbs
Lemons	2 each
Fish broth	3 pints 4 fl oz
Butter	3 ½ oz
Olive oil	3 Tbsp
Garlic	1 clove
White wine	3 ½ fl oz
Lean bacon, julienne	7 oz
Salt, Pepper, Parsley	as much as needed

Preparation

➢ In a large sauté pan put the oil and brown the minced garlic. Add the rice and toast it, bathe with the white wine and once evaporated pour in the fish broth and cook for about 15 minutes. (If you need to make your own fish stock, it is composed of: saved fish, fish bones, vegetable mirepoix, water, white wine and as much salt as you need).

➢ In the meanwhile hand wash and clean the shrimps cut them in halves lengthwise and add to the risotto, they will cook up shortly.

➢ If you have to make crispy bacon, do this early and reserve it for near the end.

➢ For purposes of cooking, add the lean bacon before jump in the butter to add polish, finish with parsley and serve with lemon wedges.

*Speak is an Italian bacon product with almost no fat. It requires little cooking time so it may be added last. Regular bacon can be substituted if it gets cooked to a crispiness that accompanies the shrimp.

**Italian prawns are so large that it easy to cut them lengthwise from nose to tail through a heavy shell.

RISOTTO ALLA VENETA

Risotto Venetian style

Serves 10

Ingredients

Arborio rice	2 lbs 7 oz
Butter	7 oz
Vegetable broth	1 quart, 19 fl oz
Salt & Pepper	as much as needed
Peas	7 oz
White wine	3 ½ fl oz
Parmesan cheese, granular	5 oz
Kitchen cream	5 fl oz
Parsley, minced	3 ½ oz
Onion, minced	3 ½ oz
Proscuitto, cut into pieces	7 oz

Preparation

➢ In a large sauté pan put the butter, heat it and add the onion.

➢ Pour in the rice and toast it, bathe in the wine and allow it to evaporate.

➢ Add the broth, a little at a time and then cook for about 10 minutes.

➢ Pour in the peas and the prosciutto and remove from heat.

➢ Cook until creamy with butter, kitchen cream and granular Parmesan cheese, dust with parsley and serve like a sudden wave.

RISOTTO MARI E MONTI

Sea and mountain risotto

Serves 10

Ingredients

Arborio rice	1 lb 10 oz
Butter	5 oz 2 tsp
Fish Stock, or Fumet	2 ½ pints
Shrimp	2 lbs
White table wine	3 ½ fl oz
Cultivated mushrooms	1 lb
Black mussels	2 lbs
Parmesan cheese, crumbs	5 oz
Olive oil	as much as needed
Cream	as much as needed
Garlic	2 oz
Parsley, minced	2 oz

Preparation

➤ To prepare the fumet use the shrimp peels and shrimp heads, some trimmings from the mushrooms, parsley stems, ½ cup white wine, and 2 pints of water. Or use a fish stock.

➤ In a large sauté pan melt the butter and brown the garlic, minced. Unite with the fresh mushrooms which you have washed and treated with love. These fresh shrimp will need to be shelled and pinch away the head from the tail. Brown the tails and continue cooking for another 5 minutes. Pour in the rice and toast it, bathe with the white wine and allow the liquid to evaporate. To cook pour in the fish broth and stir continuously for 10 minutes. Add the black mussels, for purposes of opening their shells make a shallow poaching liquid; once the shell is open they are ready to add to the risotto rice, and the poaching liquid can be added to the risotto as needed. Complete the cooking with the last of the fish broth. Cook until creamy with butter, cream, and grated parmesan cheese, sprinkle with parsley.

SPAGHETTI ALLE COZZE

Spaghetti and mussels

Serves 10

Ingredients

Black mussels	5 lbs
Olive oil	10 fl oz
Parsley	3 ½ oz
Spaghetti	2 ¼ lbs
Garlic	as much as needed
Tomato sauce	2 lbs
Pepper & salt	as much as needed

Preparation

➢ Clean the black mussels under running water of their whiskers or any sand. Open them over a high heat in a shallow pan just covered in water and unlock the shells then set aside reserved in their water.

➢ Mince the garlic, make it turn browned in the olive oil and add the mussels, some parsley, the tomato sauce, the pepper and the mussel's reserved poaching liquid. Continue cooking until the spaghetti is ready. (The tomato sauce should already be warmed by the time you add it to all these ingredients). Turn the heat down when it reaches desired consistency.

➢ Cook the spaghetti in boiling water that is salted; drain off the water when it has reached al dente. Taste the sauce with mussels and add salt if needed.

➢ Before service sprinkle with minced parsley.

SECONDE DI PESCE

Second course fish-These are fish entreés, baked, fried, cooked in a pot, marinated or grilled.

1) Mussels and clams over spaghetti. The mussels, shrimps, clams and cherry tomatoes cook until they pop open on a high heat with some olive oil and a ladle of fish stock.

2) The chief cook has prepared spaghetti with black mussels for the table of four. They have ordered a three course meal and he is just adding the finish touches to their meal.

DENTICE AL FORNO CON OLIVE

Oven baked fish with olives

*In lieu of acquiring the fresh dentice at your local fish market, fish steaks of 1 one inch thick halibut or swordfish can be used; or the thick filets of haddock or cod. Also, black olives can be substituted for the green ones.

Ingredients

Dentice	5 lbs
Olive oil	7 fl oz
Lemons	7 oz
Salt & Pepper	as much as needed
Rosemary	as much as needed
Green olives	8 oz
White wine	1 Tbsp
Bay leaf	as many as needed
Garlic	as much as needed

Preparation

➢ Clean, scale and wash by hand the dentice. Systematically in a frying pan flavor the fish with salt, the pepper, the lemon, the bay leaf and garlic.

➢ Put in the oven at 350'F in a roasting pan the fish with all the oil and flavors from the frying pan adding the olives, the chopped rosemary, cook until scarcely done and browned bathe with the white wine and only if necessary with water.

➢ Scarcely cooked, systematically place on a serving platter, pulling it apart in the roasting pan used for cooking. To the cooking juices add a little flour some water.

➢ Reduce to a consistency desired. Pour on the fish and serve.

FILETTO DI SPIGOLA AL CARTOCCIO

Foil wrapped bass fillets

Serves 10

Ingredients

Fresh Bass	5 lbs
Lemons	as many as needed
Parsley	as much as needed
Olive oil	as much as needed
Salt & Pepper	as much as needed
Leaves of aluminum foil	as many as needed

Preparation

➤ Scale, remove the guts, and filet the bass. In an orderly way, place the fillets in pieces of aluminum foil leaves, season with salt, pepper, oil and lemon juice. Wrap the foil jackets into a closed seal and cook them systematically on a baking sheet in the oven set at 400' F for about 5 minutes.

FILETTO DI SPIGOLA EN CROUTE

Baked sea bass filet & mash potatoes wrapped in bread

Mashed potatoes w/shaved green onions & shaved onion

Sea bass filet

Baguette, long fresh bread

Olive oil

Balsamic vinegar

Roma tomato

The bass is piled with a layer of mashed potatoes. Wrapped with bread from a long baguette, the bread winding two and a half times around the filet and adhering to the mashed potatoes, doused with olive oil, baked until the fish is white & flaky and the bread has the crispness of croutons. The plate is drizzled with balsamic vinegar in many points and three round slices of roma tomato to the side.

*We were served this at our resort, so I watched the cook prepare it for others. The mashed potatoes are made in advance and should still be warm; the bass filets made ready. Slicing a long baguette with a bread knife to a thickness of about one centimeter and begin by setting the filet on the bread, then potatoes and wrap around once, at a slight angle wrap twice this should about cover the potatoes, a half wrap turns the bread under. Use a toothpick to secure the bread to the potatoes on filet if need be.

MISTO DI MARE

Mixed seafood salad medley

Ingredients

Swordfish, first grilled then chopped into bite size pieces, tossed in oil & vinagrette, to dress, marinate for half hour prior to assembly

Cuddlefish, (squid) cut like bamboo shoots steamed, poached or saute

Head-on shrimp, 2 per plate, grilled or saute

Octopus, boiled whole then cut into pieces

Squid, tender calamari, light batter deep fried

A scallop and crab fritter with bistro sauce, (scallop battered and deep fried), (seasoned crab mixture rolled into a ball about 1 tsp battered deep fried).

Bistro sauce : to 2 cups mayonnaise add 2 Tbsp catsup, 2 Tbsp dijon mustard, 1 ½ Tbsp horseradish, 1 Tbsp lemon juice, 1 ½ tsp Worcestershire sauce, 1 tsp tabasco, 1 tsp cajun spice, 1 tsp paprika, 2 cloves garlic minced. Mix together in a bowl, chill until service.

Crab cake mixture: to 1 lb crab meat add 1 egg, 1 ½ Tbsp mayonnaise, 1 Tbsp Dijon mustard, 1 tsp Worcestershire sauce, salt, oil. In a small bowl combine the wet flavoring ingredients with a binder like Panko or bread crumbs. Mix together the crab meat with everything and roll into balls the size of 1 tsp meatball.

The crab fritter and scallop fritter can be made if dipped into a batter then deep fried in oil brought to 350'F. In the USA we use Drakes dry mix for a beer batter, the raw scallop can be wet from beer, rolled in flour before lightly coated in batter.

The crab fritter is a gooey mixture that fries up golden brown to dark brown. A beer batter coating will bulk it up.

We take calamari rings and wet them in buttermilk with a little hot sauce. Then toss them in flour with spices; garlic powder, seasoning salt, paprika, until the buttermilk coat dries with flour. The coated rings are deep fried for a couple minutes until they turn color and when they are crisped enough for your taste.

Assemble on salad plates. Serve as a second course-fish sampler in mostly small pieces so colorfully arranged to appear as a salad-with no onion, lettuce, or tomato needed.

The cook at the Resort Alimini Smile Villagio prepared this for our group at the first sit-down dinner. There are many small components to balance but he was able to complete the process by planning ahead of time and calculating the time needed to cook everything through.

POLPO IN PIGNATA

Octopus in a pot

Ingredients

Octopus	4 lbs
Celery, minced	3 ½ oz
Olive oil	10 fl oz
Salt & Pepper	as much as needed
Rosemary	as much as needed
Carrot, minced	3 ½ oz
Garlic	2 cloves
Olive oil	7 fl oz
Peeled tomatoes	7 oz
Oregano	as much as needed
Onion, minced	3 ½ oz

Preparation

➢ Clean, wash by hand, and carve the octopus.

➢ Take a large sauté pan, put in the oil, heat it, add the mirepoix, the garlic and make browned.

➢ Pour the octopus into the sauté pan and add the remaining above ingredients from the list and cook.

➢ Before service dust with parsley.

SPIEDINO DI CALAMARI E GAMBERI

Shrimp and Calamari Kebab

Serves 10

Ingredients

Calamari	2 lbs
Prawns, slip off shells	1 lb 3 ½ oz
Worcester sauce	as much as needed
Mustard	as much as needed
Bread, for crumbs	as much as needed
Parmesan cheese, granular	as much as needed
Salt & Pepper	as much as needed
Olive oil	as much as needed
Parsley, minced	as much as needed
Lemon juice	as much as needed

Preparation

➢ Slice the calamari into rings and prepare skewers together along with shrimp.

➢ As soon as ready place them in an orderly way in a baking dish greased with oil. Brush kebabs with mustard and Worcester.

➢ In a tureen prepare a mixture of bread crumbs, finely grated cheese, salt, pepper, oil, lemon juice and parsley.

➢ Give the skewers a light coating of this hodgepodge mixture by dusting them and bake in the oven at 400'F finish when they have turned golden colored. Take out from the oven and serve hot.

SECONDE DI CARNE

Second course meat-These are meat entreés of roast lamb, veal fillets, beef steak, spicy hot chicken and ground veal loaf hamburgers

1) Thin cuts of beef, a sprinkle of parmesan cheese, oregano, parsley, shaved ham and cubes of fontina cheese make up these meat roll-ups. Rouladen can be browned in a pan and warmed in the oven.

2) The woman helps out at the family restaurant doing whatever she needs to make a meal special. She is putting together a plate full of traditional European rouladen.

AGNELLO AL FORNO CON PATATE

Roast lamb with potatoes

Serves 10

Ingredients

Lamb	4 lbs
Potatoes	3 lbs
Olive oil	7 fl oz
Ripe tomatoes	10 oz
Garlic	1 clove
Bread crumbs	5 oz
Parmesan, grated	3 ½ oz
Salt, Pepper, Rosemary	as much as needed

Preparation

➢ Carve this lamb into pieces and brown all sides in a frying pan over a high heat.

➢ Peel the potatoes with a paring knife and slice to a thickness of one centimeter.

➢ Place the lamb in a roasting pan season with salt, pepper, rosemary, tomato pieces and minced garlic.

➢ Unite the potatoes in the roaster and cover with cold water.

➢ Cook in the oven at 400'F for an hour and a half all around.

➢ Take it out of the oven, dust with the bread crumbs and grated cheeses crumbs mixed together and return to the oven for another 20 minutes.

➢ This stew is meant to be complete when the surface has achieved a golden crust, and the depth of the cooking is dry of the water.

AMBURGHER AI FUNGHI

Ground veal hamburger with mushrooms

Serves 10

Ingredients

Veal shoulder	3 lbs
Eggs	3 each
Parmesan cheese, granular	5 oz
Champignon mushrooms	13 oz
Olive oil	3 ½ fl oz
White wine	7 fl oz
Chopped parsley	3 ½ oz
Salt & Pepper	as much as needed

*Champignons are button mushrooms.

Preparation

➢ The mushrooms are to be cooked in a traditional way with oil, garlic and parsley.

➢ Pass the meat through a meat grinder and amalgamate the ground veal with the eggs, the parmesan cheese, and the salt & pepper.

➢ Prepare hamburger patties and brown on both sides, in oil, for several minutes.

➢ In a baking dish place the hamburgers.

> ➢ Bathe in the wine and add to that the mushrooms.

> ➢ Cook in the oven at 350'F for about 5 minutes.

> ➢ Remove from the heat, systematically put on a heat-resistant platter or plate up and serve.

BOCCONCINI DI VITELLO IN UMIDO CON PISELLI

Delicacy of veal in a stew with peas

Serves 10

Ingredients

Veal shoulder	4 lbs
Brunoise, celery, carrot, onion	10 oz
Mild paprika	1 oz +1 tsp
Garlic	1 clove
Meat broth	as much as needed
Tomato paste	3 ½ oz
Peeled tomatoes	2 lbs
Peas	1 lb

Preparation

➢ Prepare a brunoise of celery, carrot, and onion very small dice as minced.

➢ Cut the meat into cubes weighing roughly 2 oz each.

➢ Heat the whole tomatoes in a pot. They should have the skin peeled away. When the tomatoes get hot, smash them into pulp & juices with either an immersion blender or food mill which takes away the seeds.

➢ Take a large sauté pan and brown the brunoise with the oil. Unite the meat, the paprika, the garlic and continue cooking for 15 minutes. Pour in the peeled tomatoes, the tomato paste and cover with the broth.

➤ Cook on a low flame for 2 hours, turning often and add another cup of broth if necessary.

➤ Add to the delicacy the peas. Continue cooking it for another 10 minutes, adjust the flavors of salt and pepper and serve very hot.

FETTA A MAIALE ALLA CAPRESE

Sliced roast pork caprese style

Ingredients

Center Loin	whole roast
Roast Pork	4 slices thin like lunchmeat
Tomatoes	half a large tomato chopped
Fresh mozzarella	4 small fresh mozzarella balls
Fresh basil	half a dozen leaves ripped

Preparation

To arrange in layers, first the pork slices to cover the plate, toss tomatoes over the meat, center the mozzarella balls, rip the leaves and throw over top. A little olive oil is okay drizzled on top.

The local butcher says to use a Center Loin cut of pork. It is boneless, and so it may be sliced into whole cuts after cooking.

The roast pork shall be best served at room temperature or after being chilled.

FILETTO DI VITELLO ALLA MAITRE D'HOTEL

Maitre d'hotel beef fillet

Serves 10

Ingredients

Beef fillets	4 lbs
Butter	5 oz
Lemon	1 each
Minced Parsley	as much as needed
Garlic	2 cloves
Salt	as much as needed

Preparation

➤ Soften the butter and make into dough combining the lemon juice and minced parsley. This makes a compound butter.

➤ With the composition being amalgamated, form a cylinder and wrap in a transparent film; make to chill in the refrigerator.

➤ Carve or trim the filets and flavor the slices with salt and minced garlic; cook in a frying pan with a little oil.

➤ Arrange the filets on a serving platter, put in the middle of every slice a washer of butter and serve immediately.

FILETTO DI VITELLO AL PEPE VERDE

Veal fillets with green peppercorns

*green peppercorns are available in some places online, their flavor is mild and the whole peppercorn is edible.

Ingredients

Veal filets	4 lbs
Brandy	2 fl oz
Butter	5 oz
Salt	as much as needed
Kitchen cream	3 ½ fl oz
Flour	as much as needed
Vegetable broth	as much as needed
Green peppercorns	2 oz

Preparation

➢ Carve or trim the veal filets into pieces weighing from 7 oz each. Using a paring knife, make little incisions and insert the green peppercorns.

➢ Tranche the filets in flour and brown in the butter on both sides, add salt.

➢ Add the brandy and flash ablaze.

➢ Unite the kitchen cream and the vegetable broth and continue the cooking for a few minutes more to create a reduced sauce.

➢ To serve cover the meat in the same sauce.

PEZZETTI DI CAVALLO

Pieces of horsemeat

*The Mediterranean people sometimes inherit the Beta-form of sickle cell anemia; local treatments include drinking horse's blood and serving horsemeat to fortify the blood of their anemic children.

Serves 10

Ingredients

Lean meat of horse	3 lbs
Chili peppers	as many as needed
Olive oil	10 fl oz
Salt & Peppercorns	as much as needed
Bay leaves	as many as needed
Tomato paste	3 Tbsp
Tomato sauce	10 oz
Minced onions	5 oz

Preparation

➤ Put the meat in a pot to boil with the peppercorns and bay leaves, cover with water. The meat may need to cook for 2 hrs on boil because it is a hard meat.

➤ Now chop the meat into pieces.

➤ Take a large sauté pan, put in the olive oil and brown the onions.

➤ Add the tomato paste and tomato sauce and make it cook for 5 minutes.

➤ Pour the meat into the sauté pan with tomato and some of the drippings and make it cook until done. It is finished when the meat is well-done.

➤ Serve in a ceramic casserole bowl.

POLLO ALLA DIAVOLA

Devilishly hot chicken

Serves 10

Ingredients

Chicken	3 lbs
Hot chili peppers	as many as needed
Olive oil	10 fl oz
Salt & pepper	as much as needed
Rosemary	as much as needed

Preparation

➢ Chop the chicken into very good pieces.

➢ Season them with these ingredients listed above and put in the oven at 400'F degrees.

➢ Take out of the oven and the roasting pan, then to serve pour the above chicken and its reserves from cooking into a large bowl where you can mix with your hands.

➢ To finalize the cooking add capers, some olives and bread crumbs. Amalgamate all-of-this together well and serve cold.

SCALLOPPE DI VITELLO PRIMAVERA

Veal scallopini with spring vegetables

Serves 10

Ingredients

Veal, lean cut	4 lbs
Pickled garden vegetables	3 ½ oz
Flour	as much as needed
Water	as much as needed
Butter	5 oz
Cooking oil	7 fl oz
Parsley, salt & pepper	as much as needed

Preparation

➢ Flatten the meat by beating it, season with salt and pepper; pass it through a tranche of flour and brown on both sides with a little oil and butter. Arrange the scallops on a buttered tray. Place the pickled vegetables on top after a fast coating in a pan with parsley, oil, butter. Keep warm in the oven on a low heat until the gravy is prepared.

➢ Take the drippings from cooking thicken with flour and thin with water, then reduce and pass it through a sieve to get out any lumps.

➢ Pour over the scallops and serve.

SCALLOPPA DI VITELLO AI FUNGHI

Veal scaloppini with mushrooms

Serves 10

Ingredients

Veal, lean cut	3 lbs
Champignon mushrooms	2 lbs
Flour	as much as needed
Water	as much as needed
Butter	5 oz
Cooking oil	7 fl oz
Parsley, salt & pepper	as much as needed

Preparation

➢ The mushrooms need to be sautéed in a little oil and butter with the parsley.

➢ Beat flat the meat, salt & pepper it; pass it through a tranche of flour and brown it on both sides with a little oil and butter. Arrange the scaloppini on a buttered tray, place the mushrooms on top. Keep warm until the gravy is ready and you are ready to serve.

➢ Pull out from the drippings by thickening with flour and thinning with water, then reduce and pass it through a sieve to remove any lumps.

➢ Pour this gravy over the scaloppini and serve.

CONTOURNI

Potatoes, tomatoes, and bell peppers, eggplant, onion, fennel bulb and zucchini comprise the vegetable dishes of the Mediterranean region.

Fresh produce like cabbage, prickly pear cactus, yellow bell peppers, cherry tomatoes, and roma tomatoes can be found in an open air market.

CIPOLLE GRATINATE

Au gratin onions

Serves 10

Ingredients

Onions, large	10 each
Pecorino cheese	1 ½ oz
Parmesan cheese	1 ½ oz
Bread crumbs	2 oz
Olive oil	2 fl oz
Broth	3 ½ fl oz
White wine	3 ½ fl oz
Salt & pepper, parsley	as much as needed

Preparation

➤ Peel the onions and chop them in half, place in a baking dish.

➤ Prepare with the cheese, the olive oil, the breadcrumbs, parsley, salt and pepper and jumble it together sprinkling it over the onions.

➤ Bathe with white wine, stretch with the broth and cook in the oven for about 20 minutes.

➤ The oven should be 375'F, the broth must come to a boil in order to cook the onions, aluminum foil is a good protective measure but turn the corners up.

FUNGHI TRIFOLATI

Mushrooms cooked in olive oil, garlic and parsley

A classic dish, this is how it is done.

Serves 10

Ingredients

Champignon mushrooms	4 lbs (button mushrooms)
Olive oil	7 fl oz
Pepper	as much as needed
Fine salt	as much as needed
Parsley, minced	as much as needed
Garlic, minced	2 cloves
White wine	3 ½ fl oz

Preparation

➤ Clean the mushrooms, hand-wash them and cut them into thin slices.

➤ Brown them in a sauté pan of garlic and some oil.

➤ Pour in the mushrooms and make to cook them finished when not so dry of all the water.

➤ Bathe them with the wine, make it evaporate and adjust the seasonings of salt and pepper.

➤ Before service sprinkle with the parsley.

PATATE AL ROSMARINO

Rosemary potatoes

Serves 10

Ingredients

Floury potatoes	3 lbs
Rosemary	as much as needed
Olive oil	2 fl oz
Salt & pepper	as much as needed
Minced garlic	as much as needed

Preparation

➤ Peel and cut the potatoes. Parboil in salted water and then arrange them in a roasting pan with the other ingredients.

➤ Cook in the oven at 400'F for about 45 minutes. Serve hot.

PATATE NOCCIOLA

Light brown potatoes

Serves 10

Ingredients

Boiling potatoes	4 lbs
Salt & pepper	as much as needed
Olive oil	3 ½ fl oz
Sage & rosemary	as much as needed

Preparation

➢ Peel the potatoes and achieve spheres using a melon baller.

➢ Be prepared to keep the potato balls in water so they remain whitened, lightly salted water bring to boil and pour potato balls into a roasting pan.

➢ Season with the rest of the ingredients and bake at 350'F for about 30 minutes.

➢ To get the potatoes browned, coat them well in the olive oil, turn them occasionally while baking; they may be wrapped in a tinfoil pouch or baked in a single layer.

PEPERONATA ALLE OLIVE NERE

Pan roasted peppers with black olives

Serves 10

Ingredients

Bell peppers, red & yellow	3 lbs
Black olives	7 oz
Olive oil	2 fl oz
Peeled tomatoes	7 oz
Salt & pepper, oregano	as much as needed
Parsley	1 ½ Tbsp
Onions	7 oz

Preparation

➢ Wash the peppers and cut them into chunks.

➢ Take a large sauté pan, put in the oil and make to brown the onions cut into julienne with the peppers.

➢ Add to it the peeled tomatoes, salt & pepper and oregano and cook for 20 minutes, paying attention to the pan so the ingredients do not burn or cook on only one side.

➢ When it is done put in the olives and sprinkle with parsley.

PEPERONI IN AGRODOLCE

Sweet and sour peppers

Serves 10

Ingredients

Yellow Bell peppers	1 5/8 lbs
Red Bell peppers	1 5/8 lbs
Red onions	1 lb
Olive oil	5 fl oz
Capers	2 oz
Green olives	4 oz
Salt & Pepper	as much as needed
Bread crumbs	as much as needed

Preparation

➢ Cut the bell peppers in large pieces. The onion should be sliced to the same size.

➢ Take a large sauté pan and heat the oil, unite the peppers together with the onions, salt once and stew everything for about 1 hour on a low flame.

➢ At the end of cooking, add the capers, the olives and bread crumbs. Mix this together well to amalgamate the flavors and serve cold.

SPINACI CON PINOLI E UVETTA

Spinach with pine nuts and raisins

Serves 10

Ingredients

Spinach	2 lbs
Butter	3 ½ oz
Pine nuts	¾ oz
Raisins	2 oz
Grated parmesan cheese	2 oz
Salt & pepper	as much as needed

Preparation

➢ Boil the spinach then drain off the water. In a sauté pan jump in with the butter, the spinach and pine nuts. Add a finely cut raisins, parmesan cheese and season with salt and pepper.

DOLCE

The dessert course can be cake, pie, custards, or sweets.

1) The gelato shoppe is the busiest place in town for tourist season. Fresh gelato is made every day and there are many wonderful flavors.

2) A simple dessert of panna cotta with strawberry syrup is served at our lunch hour.

CIAMBELLA CON RICOTTA

Ring-shaped cake with ricotta cheese

Serves 10

Ingredients

Fresh ricotta	15 oz
Flour	1 lb
Sugar	1 lb
Egg yolks	5 each
Grated lemon peel	1 lemon
Baking powder	½ tsp
Kitchen cream	3 ½ fl oz

Preparation

➢ Whip together in a bowl the ricotta with the egg yolks.

➢ Add the flour, the sugar and the yeast.

➢ Soften the dough with kitchen crème and lemon rind.

➢ Pour into a mold for ciambella that has been greased with butter and dusted with flour.

➢ Bake at 350'F.

➢ Remove from the oven when the surface is golden.

CRÈME CARAMEL

Cream caramel

Serves 10

Ingredients

Whole milk	1 ¾ pints
Sugar	10 oz
Whole eggs	10 each
Vanilla	1 ½ tsp
Caramelized sugar	7 oz

Preparation

➤ Put on to boiling all the milk and vanilla.

➤ In a bowl put the sugar, the eggs and beat them vigorously and add the milk which has been brought to boiling. In a small saucepan put the sugar with a cupful of water making it caramelize, pour the caramel in an appropriate mould, and fill with the mixture prepared proceeding to this.

➤ Systematically arrange the moulds in a container for bain-marie and cook in the oven at a moderate heat for 30 minutes.

CREMA PASTICCERA

Pastry cream

Makes 3 lbs

Ingredients

Eggs	6 each
Sugar	10 oz
Flour	10 oz
Heavy cream	1 pint 12 oz

Preparation

➤ Mix together the eggs and sugar, and then add the flour. Meanwhile, heat the milk to boiling. Add the hot milk to the composition, first about one third and stir it together. Then pour the composition back in with the remaining milk and put it on the heat again.

➤ Bring it to a second boil for about 2 minutes. Chill it in the refrigerator until needed.

CROSTATA ALLA FRUTTA

Fruit crostata

Serves 10

Ingredients

Pasta frolla	1 lb
Crema pasticcera	1 lb
Fresh fruit of the season	as much as needed
Gelatin	as much as needed

Preparation

➢ Line a 9 inch drop out bottom tart pan (or a pie tin) with the pasta frolla. The crust is baked empty, until firm and golden. Knock it out and fill it with pastry cream.

➢ Decorate with fresh fruit and gloss with transparent gelatin.

➢ Suggested fruit topping, apples, kiwi and brandied cherry on top.

CROSTATA ALLA MARMELLATA D'ALBICOCCA

Apricot jam tart

Serves 10

Ingredients

Flour	18 oz
Butter	10 oz
Eggs	2 egg yolks + 1 whole egg
Lemon zest	from 1 lemon
Vanilla	1 ½ tsp
Baking powder	2 tsp
Salt	a pinch
Apricot jam	1 lb
Sugar	7 oz

Preparation

➤ Sift the flour and place on your work table making a fountain.

➤ In the well of the fountain add the sugar, softened butter that is nearly liquid, the grated lemon zest, the vanilla; a pinch of salt, the baking powder, and eggs then mix it delicately until it combines into unified dough.

➤ Leave it to rest in the refrigerator covered with a linen napkin for a half hour.

➤ Take the dough from the refrigerator and stretch it, roll it to a thickness of one half centimeter (> ¼ inch). Some dough will be needed to trim the surface of the crostata in a cross hatch weave, reserve any leftover pieces of dough to roll out in stripes.

➤ Take a tart dish with a drop out bottom, grease it to prevent sticking and dust with a minimum amount of flour; then arrange the dough to fit. Trim the dough to the height of the tart dish with a knife, reserve the trimmings.

➤ Poke the tart shell with a fork to let air escape while baking. Bake at 350'F for 15 minutes. This will be enough time to let the crust set.

➤ Allow the shell to cool off before filling with jam, spread the apricot jam to fit in the shell. It is okay to use less jam.

➤ Roll out the reserved dough to a thin 1/8 inch if possible and garnish the crostata with stripes of dough in a cross hatch weave. Take a beaten egg and water to make egg wash and brush the crust and cross hatch dough with egg wash.

➤ Bake in the oven for about 15 minutes at a temperature of 350'F. Check to see if the crust is done before pulling from the oven.

OBAMA-THE PASTICCIOTTO

Traditional Italian pastry reformulated in cocoa & chocolate

Pasta frolla

All purpose flour	10oz
Sugar	5 oz
Butter	5 oz
Eggs	1 each
Egg yolks	1 each
Cocoa powder	2 oz

Crema pasticceria

Half and half	1 liter
Sugar	250 g
Egg yolks	8 each
Flour	120 g
Vanilla	1 tsp
Chocolate	2 oz

Procedure

To make the dough, begin with softened butter and the egg and extra egg yolk. Cream together in a bowl with a mixer and add the sugar, cocoa and flour. Let the dough just come together before taking it from the bowl and kneading it so it comes together in a neat ball. Wrap the dough in plastic and let it rest in the refrigerator for a half hour before using it to make two pie shells; roll it out for a pie top and bottom. Grease a pie pan and dust with flour then fold the bottom part in and make it to fit.

The pastry cream must be cooked, so begin by combining the wet ingredients together in a medium to large pot off the heat. Pour in the half and half, eggs, vanilla and the sugar-whisk the mixture until the sugar is all dissolved and add the flour in parts. For example, add one quarter of the flour to the wet mixture and stir in.

Place the pot on low heat and warm the mixture, whisk the flour into the solution to remove lumps. Begin a slow cooking process and add the second quarter flour, whisk almost constantly then add the third and fourth quarters of the flour. Increase the heat so it comes to a slow boil. It should cook just at boiling for 25 minutes. A nice pastry cream will cook out the taste of flour and still be sticky. Add the chocolate last, while the pastry cream is hot and swirl it around to make even. Let the pastry cream rest a little while to cool down before pouring it into the shell and covering with the top shell. Trim the crust edges or crimp them with a fork. Bake the cream filled pie at 350'F for a half hour, pull from the oven,

When US President Obama visited Italy for the first time after a major earthquake event, some Italian bakers made in honor of his visit a favorite Italian dessert and changed the formula slightly so it was a chocolate version with a cocoa crust. In small Italian pastry shops, the traditional pasticiotto, and its variations, including the Obama pasticiotto are baked in small cookie molds about two inches long and an inch wide in an oval half moon shape.

PASTA FROLLA

Pasta frolla is typical pastry dough

Yield: 1 lb pastry dough

Ingredients

Semolina flour	10 oz
Sugar	5 oz
Butter	5 oz
Eggs	1 each
Egg yolks	1 each
Lemon zest	½ lemon

Procedure

➢ On a flat surface, take your available flour and make a fountain with hole in the center for other ingredients. Sprinkle with your sugar and the salt and take care with the means of softened butter, an egg, an egg yolk and the grated peel of half a lemon.

➢ Amalgamate quickly the ingredients, throwing the sides towards the center. The secret for a good pasta frolla is working the dough for as short a time as possible, adding a little lukewarm water to hold together from breaking apart.

➢ Form a ball and allow it to rest for an hour in a cool place wrapped in a cloth.

TARTELLETTE ALLA FRUTTA

Cream filled fruit tartlet

Serves 10

Ingredients

Pasta frolla	1 lb
Pastry cream	1 lb
Fresh fruit in season	as much as needed
Gelatin	as much as needed

Preparation

➤ Line with the pasta frolla the mold for a tartlet. Cook it empty, take it from the oven and fill it with pastry cream.

➤ Decorate with fresh fruit and polish with transparent gelatin.

TIRAMISU

Italian expresso cake

Serves 10

Ingredients

Whole eggs, separated	10 each
Castor sugar	10 oz
Mascarpone cheese	1 lb
Whipping cream	1 lb
Bitter cocoa	as much as needed
Expresso coffee	as much as needed
Lady fingers	40 each

Preparation

> ➤ The mascarpone cheese will be mixed with three components to form a light, soft icing. First, whip 10 egg yolks with 5 oz of sugar. Proceed to incorporate the mascarpone cheese into the sweetened egg yolks. Take the whipping cream and whip into foam about double in volume. Fold in the whipped cream and last cream 10 egg whites with 5 oz sugar to soft peaks and fold in, too.

> ➤ Set out 10 dessert dishes and assemble in layers.

> ➤ Soak two ladyfingers in expresso and place in dessert dish. Do not delay in retrieving them from the caffe or the delicate cakes will fall apart when you pick them up.

> ➤ Pile a large scoop of icing on the expresso saturated ladyfingers and spread smooth. Sprinkle with cocoa powder. Make a second layer.

> ➤ Keep chilled prior to service.

TORTA MIMOSA

Mimosa pineapple cake

*Bagna – strong liquor used to flavor pastries, or pastry cream

Serves 10

Ingredients

Whole eggs	10 each
Castor sugar	10 oz
Cake flour	10 oz
Whipped cream	1 lb
Pastry cream	1 lb
Bagna	½ tsp
Pineapple in syrup	1 lb
Yeast	½ tsp
Candied cherries	for decorating

Preparation

➢ Put in a mixing bowl the eggs, the sugar and bring them up until doubled their initial volume.

➢ Take away and incorporate slowly the flour and the yeast which you have just sifted. Pour the mixture into a cake tin that is buttered and dusted with flour and put in the oven at 325'F for about 20 minutes.

➢ Take it out of the oven and let it cool off, and slice the sponge cake in half.

➢ Bathe the cake with the pineapple's syrup and the splash.

➢ In a tureen, blend the pastry cream. The whipped cream and pieces of pineapple.

➢ Pour all of it over the sponge cake, level it with a spatula, work it into the shape of a dome and complete with crumbs from the sponge cake.

➢ Decorate with whipped cream and candied cherries.

TORTA PASTICCIOTTO

Pastry cream baked in a pie

*Traditionally pasticciotto have a standard size and oval shape from pastry molds used in bakeshops across the Salento region. There are many variations to filling, topping, and flavors.

Serves 10

Ingredients

Pasta frolla	2 lbs
Pastry cream	2 ½ pints
Sugar, to veil	as much as needed

Preparation

➢ Roll out the pastry dough to a thickness of 1 cm and line a torte pan with the dough, one that has been buttered and floured.

➢ Pour the pastry cream into the torte shell and cover with another layer of pastry dough having the same thickness.

➢ Polish the surface with egg yolk and bake at 350'F for about 20 minutes.

➢ Remove the pie from the torte pan when it has cooled and sprinkle the surface with a veil of granulated sugar.

MENÙ DEL GIORNO

Primo a scelta:
Trofie alla Viennese
Linguine al tonno

Secondi a scelta:
Straccetti con rucola e grana
Caprese

½ lt acqua e ¼ lt di vino

Buon appetito

MENÙ DEL GIORNO

Primo a scelta:

Tagliatelle ai funghi

Risotto ai frutti di mare

Secondi a scelta:

Petto di pollo alla griglia

Orata alla brace

½ lt acqua e ¼ lt di vino

Buon appetito

MENÙ DEL GIORNO

Primo a scelta:

Gnocchi burro e salvia

Orrecchiette con salsiccia e funghi

Secondi a scelta:

Bracciola alla brace con contourno

Petto di pollo alla griglia con contourno

½ lt acqua e ¼ lt di vino

€ 14,00

MENU DEL GIORNO

Primo a scelta:

Spaghetti con crema di carciofi

Fusilli al ragu

Secondi a scelta:

Grigliata mista di carne

Frittura di pesce

1/2 lt acqua, ¼ lt di vino e caffè

€ 16,00

Buon appetito

MENÙ DEL GIORNO

Primo a scelta:
Spaghetti alle cozze
Melanzane alla parmigiana

Secondi a scelta
Filetto di orate
Straccetti con rucola e grana

½ lt acqua e ¼ lt vino

Buon appetito

CONVERSION TABLES

Weights		*Liquids*		*Oven temperatures*		
5g	¼ oz	15ml	½fl oz	110'C	225'F	gas mark ¼
15g	½ oz	25ml	1fl oz	120'C	250'F	gas mark ½
20g	¾ oz	50ml	2fl oz	140'C	275'F	gas mark 1
25g	1 oz	75ml	3fl oz	150'C	300'F	gas mark 2
50g	2oz	100ml	3 ½fl oz	160'C	325'F	gas mark 3
75g	3oz	125ml	4fl oz	180'C	350'F	gas mark 4
125g	4oz	150ml	¼ pint	190'C	375'F	gas mark 5
150g	5oz	175ml	6fl oz	200'C	400'F	gas mark 6
175g	6oz	200ml	7fl oz	220'C	425'F	gas mark 7
200g	7 oz	250ml	8fl oz	230'C	450'F	gas mark 8
250g	8oz	275ml	9fl oz	240'C	475'F	gas mark 9
275g	9oz	300ml	½ pint			
300g	10 oz	325ml	11fl oz			
325g	11oz	350ml	12fl oz			
375g	12oz	375ml	13fl oz			
400g	13oz	400ml	14fl oz			
425g	14oz	450ml	¾ pint			
475g	15oz	475ml	16fl oz			
500g	1lb	500ml	17fl oz			
625g	1 ¼ lb	550ml	18fl oz			
750g	1 ½ lb	600ml	1 pint			

INDEX OF RECIPES

Agnello al forno con patate.. 85

Agnoletti alla piemontese... 44

Amburgher ai funghi... 87

Arancini...18, 26, 33

Bocconcini di vitello in umido con piselli.. 89

Bruschette... 15, 18, 28, 131

Carpaccio di salmone... 29

Ciambella con ricotta... 109

Ciceri e tria... 47

Cipolle gratinate... 12, 100

Cocktail di gamberetti... 30

Crema pasticcera.. 111

Crostata alla frutta.. 112

Dentice al forno con olive.. 6, 76

Farfalle carbonara...51

Fetta a maiale alla caprese.. 91

Filetto di spigola al cartoccio... 12, 77

Filetto di spigola en croute.. 78

Filetto di vitello al pepe verde... 93

Funghi trifolati..101

Gnocchi di patate al gorgonzola.. 53

Impasto per pizza napoletana.. 31

Insalata di polpo... 12, 32

Lasagne alla bolognese... 55

Linguine agli scampi... 9, 58

Misto di mare.. 33, 79

Misto riso.. 59

Obama.. 115, 116, 132

Orecchiette alla Leccese 60

Paglia e fieno alla Bolognese... 63

Pasta frolla.. 8, 112, 115, 117, 118, 122

Pasticciotto... 115, 122, 132, 133

Patate al rosmarino..102

Patate nocciola..103

Peperoni in agrodolce 9, 105

Pezzetti di cavallo..14, 94

Pitta di patate 11, 35

Pollo alla diavola 95

Polpo in pignata 9, 81

Risotto ai gamberi e limone.. 67

Risotto ai gamberi e speak.. 68

Risotto alla veneta 70

Spaghetti alle cozze 12, 73

Spiedino di calamari e gamberi 82

Spinaci con pinoli e uvetta... 106

Tiramisu 119, 133

Torta mimosa... 11, 120

Torta pasticciotto 122, 131

Verdura in crosta..131

Zuppe di cozze con crostini... 41, 131

APPENDIX

A)
Apricot jam tart

B)
Beef, Maitre d'hotel
Bruschette, toasted garlic bread and tomato salsa

C)
Cake, ring cake with ricotta
Chicken devilishly hot
Chickpeas with pasta & wontons in broth
Cream caramel
Crostata, fruit topped

D)
Dough, shortbread pie crust

E)
Eggplant parmesan

F)
Fava bean spread with wild chicory
Fish, baked whole with olives
Fish, bass fillet wrapped in foil
Fish, sea bass fillet en croute

G)
Gnocchi, potato dumplings in creamy gorgonzola

H)
Hamburger with mushrooms, ground veal
Horsemeat, stewed

K)
Kebab, shrimp and calamari

L)
Lamb with potatoes
Lasagna classic Italian style
Linguine with prawns

M)
Mushrooms, cooked in oil

O)
Obama, pasticciotto with chocolate pastry cream
Octopus in a pot
Octopus salad
Onions, au gratin

P)
Pasta, carbonara bowties
Pasta piedmont style
Pasta, yellow and green bolognese
Pasta, in amatriciana sauce
Pasta, orecchiette with flavors of Lecce
Pastry cream
Pasticciotto, a traditional Salento pastry
Peppers, red & yellow pan-roasted
Peppers, sweet & sour
Pizza, dough and Napolese style topping
Pork, roast sliced caprese style
Potatoes, double crusted
Potatoes, light brown
Potatoes, rosemary

R)
Rice balls, deep fried
Rice salad, cold
Risottino, specialty risotto with mushrooms, bacon, and arugula
Risotto with shrimp and lemon
Risotto with bacon and shrimp
Risotto Venetian style, creamy

Risotto, sea & mountain

S)
Salmon carpaccio
Seafood, mixed medley
Seafood, salad
Shrimp cocktail
Soup, mussels and toast
Spaghetti and mussels
Spinach with pine nuts and raisins

T)
Tartlette, cream filled with fruit
Tiramisu, expresso dessert cake
Torte mimosa, pineapple topped
Torte pasticciotto, traditional cream filled

V)
Veal fillets with green peppercorns
Veal scallopini with spring vegetables
Veal scallopini with mushrooms
Veal stew with peas
Vegetable pie

WORKS CITED

Jenkins, Nancy Harmon. *Flavors of Puglia*. Pugliesi: Congedo Editore 2006-Galatina (Le), 2006. Print. traditional recipes from the heel of Italy's boot

Mangia, Corrado. "Corso intensivo di Cucina Regionale." *Progetto "Marco Polo"* (Fall 2009): 1-51. Print. IPSSART OTRANTO, Istituto Professionale di Stato per i Servizi Alberghieri, della Ristorazione e per il Turismo OTRANTO